A guide to habitat creation

THE LONDON ECOLOGY UNIT
Director: Dr D.A. Goode, BSc, FLS

The London Ecology Unit provides an ecological service
to local authorities and other agencies in London on all
aspects of nature conservation and applied ecology. The
Unit reports to, and is funded by, the London Ecology
Committee which includes most of the London Boroughs,
together with the Countryside Commission, Nature
Conservancy Council. Herts and Middlesex Wildlife
Trust and London Wildlife Trust. Its work includes the
development of ecological policies, the assessment of the
nature conservation values of sites, and the provision of
advice on appropriate management to encourage wildlife
within the capital. The Unit initiated and maintains an
ecological data-base for the London area and carries out
research as a support for its advice on urban ecology.
Much of the Unit's work involves new approaches to
nature conservation within urban areas with an emphasis
on social and economic benefits. The London Ecology
Unit also promotes greater public awareness of ecological
issues.

A series of publications is produced by the London
Ecology Unit on various aspects of its work:

1. *Ecology and Nature Conservation in London*
2. *A Guide to Habitat Creation* (1st edition out of print
    and replaced by this revised edition)
3. *Nature Conservation Guidelines for London* (out
    of print)
4. *A Nature Conservation Strategy for London:
    Woodland, Wasteland, the Tidal Thames and two
    London Boroughs* (Barnet, Lewisham)
5. *A Nature Conservation Strategy for London; the
    London Borough of Brent*
6. *Nature Conservation in Local Planning*
7. *Nature Conservation in Hillingdon*
8. *London's Meadows and Pastures*
9. *Nature Conservation in Croydon*
10. *Nature Conservation in Greenwich*
11. *Nature Conservation in Waltham Forest*
12. *Nature Conservation in Southwark*
13. *Nature Conservation in Harrow*
14. *Nature Areas for City People*
15. *Nature Conservation in Hounslow*

Copies of the handbooks are available from:
**London Ecology Unit, Bedford House,
125 Camden High Street, London NW1 7JR.**
Telephone enquiries: 071-267 7944
or from the publisher of this volume

A guide to habitat creation

Chris Baines
and
Jane Smart

A London Ecology Unit Publication

PACKARD PUBLISHING LIMITED
CHICHESTER

© 1991 The London Ecology Unit

This publication is a revised edition in a new format of a booklet of the same title published by the former Greater London Council in 1984. This edition is published for the London Ecology Unit by Packard Publishing Limited, 16 Lynch Down, Funtington, Chichester, West Sussex PO18 9LR, UK.

ISBN 1 85341 031 4

A CIP catalogue record for this book is available from the British Library.

Printed and bound in Portugal

Contents

Preface

It is now seven years since the first edition of *A guide to habitat creation* was published. The book has been extremely popular; requests for it have come from as far afield as the Isle of Skye and the United States of America. Demand for the book is as great as ever and I therefore have great pleasure in presenting this revised reprint on behalf of the London Ecology Committee.

Numerous exciting habitat-creation projects have been completed in London since the first edition was printed. Camley Street natural park, just a short walk from Kings Cross, is perhaps the best known. It has been magically transformed in just a few years from a potential lorry park into a flourishing nature reserve. It is internationally famous and receives visitors from all over the world. Other projects underway include the development of a wildlife park and ecology centre in the London Borough of Sutton, the creation of a huge wetland at South Norwood in Croydon and the development of a tree nursery in Southwark by the London Wildlife Trust.

Sadly, meadows, woodlands, hedgerows and wetlands are still disappearing from the countryside. Fortunately, however, a great many opportunities remain for the creation of new places for wildlife: gardens, parks, so-called derelict land and school grounds are all areas where wildlife habitats can be created. Even minor changes in the way we manage small areas like gardens can be of positive value to wildlife. We cannot easily recreate all the habitats that have been lost from the countryside, but we can make a significant contribution to the wildlife around us in town or city.

There is now no doubt about the increasingly widespread public support and enthusiasm which exists for nature conservation. What is lacking in some cases is the knowledge necessary to get new projects going. I hope that by reprinting this handbook on habitat creation the London Ecology Unit will continue to stimulate greater awareness of the possibilities for habitat creation and at the same time provide the technical know-how to make new ventures successful.

John Austin-Walker
Chair, London Ecology Committee

Chapter 1
Introduction

Nature conservation has traditionally been concerned with protecting places of great wildlife value, and there is no doubt about the need for such protection in the face of agricultural intensification and other pressures of new developments. But in recent years there has been a distinct swing towards a new approach which involves creating completely new habitats in places where there is at present little wildlife. This is particularly appropriate in urban areas where habitat creation is now becoming widely accepted as a crucial part of nature conservation. Many voluntary groups are now involved in this kind of work, often in close collaboration with local authorities and other official agencies. These groups have realised the many opportunities which exist for nature in all sorts of places within town and cities.

At present it is the 'unofficial' open spaces which provide wildlife habitats in urban areas. Overgrown railway sidings, revegetated derelict or vacant sites, abandoned quarries, obsolete sewage lagoons; these are the places which cater for a wide variety of species, some of which may be quite unexpected in towns. These places need careful and appropriate management and enhancement. But it is the vast areas of 'official landscapes' which offer the greatest opportunities for creating new habitats. So many of our public parks, school grounds, hospitals, college and office landscapes are relatively poor in wildlife. It is these places with their close mown grass and forlorn standard trees which offer enormous scope. The opportunities are considerable, especially for creative use of such areas by official bodies. The perimeter of a town park could be converted to a wildflower meadow, or a linear park along a river might offer the opportunity to recreate a stretch of alder woodland. Drainage authorities might create other new riverine habitats in association with their land drainage improvement works. Unused land within the railway network might be converted into new woodland or wetland. On a smaller scale gardens, hedgerows, suburban roadside verges, factory car-park shrubberies, old boundary ditches and other pockets of old landscape which have somehow survived in our cities offer great possibilities for improvement by individuals, schools and local groups.

In all of this work one of the basic principles is to reintroduce native species of British wildlife to towns and cities. Native plants tend to support a much greater variety of animal life than species introduced from other countries (Appendix 2). Plants native to Britain are preferable to the cultivars and varieties of exotic plants and trees so often used in urban landscaping.

If we can use our green spaces to sustain meadow flowers, grassland birds such as the skylark, wetland insects such as dragonflies, hedgehogs and colourful cornfield weeds, life will be far more pleasant for people living in towns. Children enjoy learning about nature. Spiders' webs daisy chains and jam jars full of tadpoles are an important part of childhood, and schools need safe accessible wild places to visit and to care for. Within school grounds the odd log pile, a nettle patch or a pond offer opportunities for habitat creation. There could be a wild sanctuary within a few minutes walk of every school. Well signed walk and cycleways could provide for 'country walks' throughout the urban landscape. There could also be pockets of land free from public disturbance where the more timid creatures can survive.

Most people in Britain live in towns, and new habitats could provide the 'countryside experience' for future generations. The tasks of management and interpretation could afford enjoyable occupations for very many people. Renewed familiarity with urban wildlife amongst townspeople may also hold the key to conservation in the wider

9

countryside. Contact with 'nature on the doorstep' must surely lead to greater and more active concern for the precious and irreplaceable habitats like ancient woodlands and bogs which are under enormous pressure.

There is another reason for adopting a more natural style of management in urban open spaces. The intensively maintained landscapes of close-mown grass and standard trees are expensive and in some ways wasteful. Labour-intensive husbandry has been replaced by machinery and chemicals and the landscape quality has tended to suffer. Times are changing and with fewer industrial manufacturing jobs, and much more leisure time, a more labour-intensive approach to landscape management could make a great deal of sense in both economic and ecological terms. Fuel oil, fertilizers and high technology all depend on the exploitation of non-renewal resources. The wild green spaces of our towns and cities offer an opportunity to use low-technology methods, occupy larger numbers of people and at the same time produce a far more interesting and valuable landscape for future generations of both wildlife and people.

In all this work it is important to remember that it is now illegal to uproot any wild plant under the terms of the *Wildlife and Countryside Act* 1981. Plants from commercial horticulturists should be used for habitat creation, unless it is possible to obtain stock from sites about to be destroyed, or from others where habitat management results in surplus material.

Chapter 2
Grasslands

In recent years many species-rich wildflower meadows have been destroyed in Britain. Although we cannot recreate communities identical to those which have been lost, colourful flowery hay meadows can be produced in about two years from scratch. Simple changes in management could create thousands of hectares of wildflower meadows in parks, around schools, along road verges, and in lots of other sterile green landscapes. This chapter describes ways of changing established grasslands into flowery meads, and also describes the alternative of starting from scratch.

Close-mown municipal grassland has little value for wildlife. By contrast, longer grass provides a rich habitat for a wide range of plants and animals.

We spend hundreds of millions of pounds every year maintaining sterile close-mown municipal grasslands. At the same time, our romantic image of the countryside is one of colourful wildflower meadows, grasshoppers and butterflies. The opportunity for creating and managing species-rich grassland communities in towns extends to hundreds of thousands of acres, and success is quick and easy to achieve. Of course we must continue to shave our sports pitches, and suburban roadside verges must be kept neat and tidy, but a more imaginative management of perhaps 20% of our urban grassland would contribute enormously to nature conservation. It would make our parks, highway verges and civic landscapes far more interesting and it could save a great deal of money.

Three principal factors determine the wildlife value of meadows. The fertility, drainage and aspect of the soil; the availability of species suited to colonisation; and the pattern of cropping management.

Adapting existing grasslands

The most colourful wildflower communities can best be developed on poor, well-drained soils. If there is an old, weedy, impoverished area of the park, or a long-neglected lawn in the hospital

Weedy old lawns on low-fertility soils are one of the best places to encourage wildflowers.

grounds, that is the place to start. Grasslands on rich soils and grasslands on wet soils are both of great value to wildlife of course, but they are far more difficult to cope with in an urban context. Poor grasslands, however, can be promoted as valuable wildflower meadows almost instantly, and fit quite happily into the resource structure of a local authority.

Mowing regimes

Grassland communities must be cropped. It is the pattern of management which determines grassland quality. If a meadow is simply abandoned, it will develop into scrubland remarkably quickly. Different mowing regimes will favour particular plants, and these in turn will provide the food for various highly selective insect larvae and other invertebrates. Rough grass will afford more cover for wildlife than a close-cropped sward, and so provide a better habitat for small mammals, larger insects, and consequently a more profitable hunting ground for predators such as the hedgehog, the kestrel, the barn owl and the stoat. It is particularly worth remembering that plant diversity will inevitably result in animal diversity. Plants are the basic platform on which the whole food web depends. Many of the invertebrates are very selective about the vegetation they eat, and a wider choice of

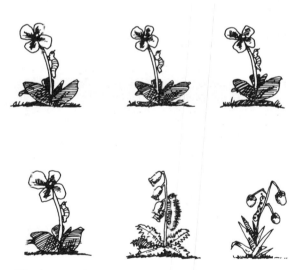

The larvae of most of our butterflies and other plant-eating invertebrates are very specific about what they eat. Increase the diversity of native food plants, and the animal life will diversify, too.

plant species will cater for a wider range of caterpillars and other larvae. The small skipper butterfly, for example, feeds only on the leaves of a couple of meadow grass species during its larval stage. The common blue butterfly must have the leaves of birdsfoot trefoil *(Lotus corniculatus)**, clover *(Trifolium* spp.*)* or black medick *(Medicago lupulina)* on which to lay its eggs and most other species of moth, beetle and butterfly have larvae which are equally choosy.

Several different management regimes seem to be appropriate for urban areas. If practicable, a variety of different mowing cycles should be adopted, but it is critical that each area of grassland enjoys its own particular pattern of cropping year after year. A change in the regime will be likely to reduce the species range.

*Nomenclature follows Clapham, Tutin and Warburg (1981) for vascular plants

1 Flowery formal lawns

Some of our most colourful and persistent wildflowers do thrive on frequent close mowing. Many of the rosette plants, for example, are all too familiar to greenkeepers and gardeners dreaming of immaculate velvet lawns. Typical plants of this particular meadow community are daisy *(Bellis perennis)*, the plantains *(Plantago* spp.*)*, cat's ear *(Hypochoeris radicata)* and low creeping plants such as speedwell *(Veronica chamaedrys)*, self-heal *(Prunella vulgaris)*, white clover *(Trifolium repens)* and birdsfoot trefoil *(Lotus corniculatus)*. This community can be enhanced by continuing to mow at regular and frequent intervals (normally every 10-14 days throughout the growing season

Once the 'weeds' have flowered, mow again and remove the clippings.

A short summer break in the mowing cycle will allow many of the rosette species to bloom.

with mower blades raised by perhaps half an inch), and most importantly, by inserting at least one gap of four to five weeks into the mowing pattern sometime in early summer. This will allow the flowers to bloom and set seed. Avoid all use of fertilizers and herbicides, and remove the clippings religiously. If they are simply allowed to lie, soil fertility will build up, and this will tend to favour a few coarse grasses and disadvantage the colourful wildflowers.

2 Springtime wildflower meadows
Many of our most attractive old meadows were cut for hay in early summer, and then grazed by cattle until well into the winter. The last few precious fritillary *(Fritillaria meleagris)* meadows are still managed this way. Adoption of this regime will very conveniently allow for recreational kickabout and picnicking, if the hay crop is taken off before the school summer holidays. The grassland should be left uncut until late June. A range of flowers and several of the more charming grasses will have time to bloom and shed ripe seed by then. At the end of June the sward should be cut down to about 50mm (2 ins) and the 'crop' removed. Ideally, the cut stems should

be left to dry as hay, and then raked up and taken away. On large areas tractor-mounted hay rakes and balers can be used, whilst on small areas school groups can have great fun tossing and then raking up the hay for use as fodder or bedding in City Farms. Hay from Hampstead Heath is fed to the Metropolitan police horses – and they actually seem to prefer it to flower-free hay. One attraction of hay-making is that it favours the shedding of ripe wildflower seed, and so speeds up the development of the meadow. If fire is a serious threat, or if labour simply cannot be organised, then an alternative for large areas is forage-harvesting. Again agricultural machinery is used, but the grass is cut and carted away either as a green crop suitable for silage production or as green bales. If the hay is fed to animals in stalls, the seed which falls out of the manger can be collected and used for new meadow sowing.

In most summers the hay stubble will recover rapidly, and the 'aftermath' which would traditionally have been grazed, may either be cut regularly throughout the rest of the season (boxing the clippings if possible) or left to grow for a second hay or silage crop in September. Spring meadows are the perfect habitat for spring bulbs such as snowdrop and daffodil of course, and typical wildflowers could include cowslips *(Primula veris)*, bugle *(Ajuga reptans)* and daisy *(Bellis perennis)*.

SPRING MEADOW.

*Leave uncut until
late June or early July.*

July

A spring meadow will support colourful wildflowers and still allow for summer kickabouts. Typical species might

3 Summer meadows

Some meadow flowers have tall stems and bloom late in summer. Field scabious *(Knautia arvensis)*, knapweed *(Centaurea scabiosa)*, hardheads *(Centaurea nigra)*, ox-eye daisy *(Leucanthemum vulgare)* and sorrel *(Rumex acetosa)* are typical examples. These plants thrive best if their meadow is left uncut from June until mid-September or later. The flowers will attract many colourful butterflies, grateful for this late summer supply of nectar. Regular cutting in the first half of the year will help prevent dominance by the coarse grasses, since their main period of leaf production will be complete by June. Again results will be most dramatic if the build-up of soil fertility is avoided by removing all the clippings. Late-summer weather can be rather wet which can make harvesting of the hay crop difficult. However, school groups may be particularly enthusiastic at this early stage in the school year, and as a last resort the forage harvester can again be employed.

Any variation on the above themes will encourage wildflowers. The essential ingredient is a break from regular mowing to allow for flowering and seed ripening. If the soil is poor, and the cuttings are removed, so much the better.

Mow and rake off the hay.   *Mow regularly at 100mm high or leave to grow for a second crop.*

August

include cowslip, bugle, milkmaids, daisy, cat's ear and selfheal.

Introducing wildflowers to established grasslands

Adoption of a sympathetic mowing regime on established grasslands will encourage certain broadleaved plants already growing. In the case of an old weedy lawn, or a recently acquired patch of old meadow this can produce spectacular results very quickly. There is no magic involved however. If your existing grassland has a poor range of wildflowers to start with, the range will not suddenly be increased by a change in mowing regime. New species can be introduced, but it is quite a complicated business. Three conditions must be satisfied. You must create a gap in the existing sward (this is one of the contributions made by grazing cattle through trampling in rural meadows). You must introduce species which have a flowering and fruiting season compatible with the adopted mowing regime. New species must also be introduced in a form which will establish rapidly, before the sward closes over the gap and swamps them out. Several alternative techniques can be adopted.

SUMMER MEADOW.

Mow regularly at 75-100mm high throughout the spring.

A summer meadow is especially good for the taller wildflowers and for breeding butterflies.

1 Over seeding

Simply scattering wildflower seed over an established sward is a waste of time. You must

Sowing directly onto an established sward is a waste of time.

create gaps in the 'canopy' if the seed is to stand a chance of germinating and establishing successfully. Physical 'scarifying' is one way of improving the chances. Ripping away at the surface, either with a spiked harrow or a steel rake, will break up the mat of dead grass and

Leave uncut from July until late September to encourage tall wildflowers.

| July | September | Take off the hay. |

Typical species might include field scabious, hardheads, knapweed and cranesbill.

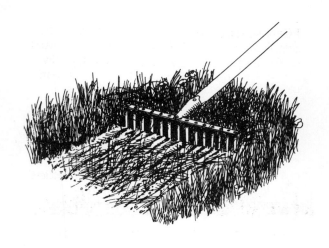

Break through the sward with a metal rake or a tractor-mounted spiked harrow.

scratch out gaps, exposing the soil. If this process rakes up a lot of matted debris, ideally this should be removed. It works best on relatively recently established grassland – say up to five or six years old. At this stage the grasses still have gaps between them.

Alternatively, chemicals can be employed to open up the sward. Of course there is an important ethical question here. Should we be employing herbicides to enhance wildflower diversity? Where 'diversification' of modern artificial grasslands is concerned, it is perhaps an acceptable means to an end. The technique is relatively simple. Either spray the area to be 'diversified' with a selective contact herbicide

Selective herbicides can be used to open up the sward for overseeding with wildflower seed and fine grasses.

which favours broadleaved plants and kills grasses (a propizamid or dalapon based herbicide would be suitable). Alternatively spray small discrete areas with a non-selective contact herbicide which will kill off both grasses and broadleaved plants, leaving gaps in the sward which can be oversown. (The current choice here is between a paraquat-based herbicide, which will kill the green parts of the plants leaving the roots unaffected, or a glyphosate-based herbicide which will kill the sward completely, roots and all).

Whichever technique is adopted, it is advisable to experiment on a relatively small area first. Timing is important. Ideally fresh seed should be sown in September, following a spray of chemical in August. Alternatively, commercial seed can be sown in April, but the sward will close over more quickly at this time of year, and certain species, most notably cowslip *(Primula veris)* are unlikely to germinate successfully.

2 Introduction by planting
Where nursery facilities exist, or the budget allows for buying in, wildflowers are probably most successfully introduced into established grasslands as small pot-grown seedlings. Again the species must be carefully chosen to suit the mowing regime, soil type and so on. Seedlings

Wildflowers appropriate to the soil type and mowing regime can be grown from seed in pots or trays and planted directly into the existing grassland.

should be introduced in groups and planted at 300-500 mm (1ft–1ft 6ins) centres A bulb-planter or trowel can be used to remove a plug of turf, and the pot-grown seedling can be introduced. Autumn planting appears to be the most successful, allowing time for the roots to become established before strong competition builds up in the following Spring. Large quantities of seedlings can be grown in trays, rather than in individual pots. It is important to emphasise the point that such introductions will quickly disappear if the subsequent mowing regime is incompatible.

3 Introduction by turf

Initially, the introduction of plants as seed or seedlings diversifies only the vegetation. Certainly the more mobile invertebrates will find a new colony of specific food plants surprisingly quickly. Wandering common-blue butterflies will sometimes settle and breed on trefoil seedlings in the first

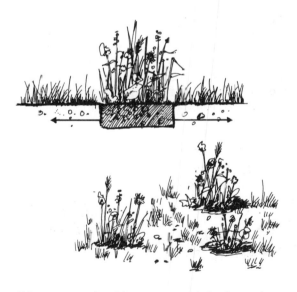

If fragments of turf from an established meadow are transplanted into the species-poor sward, resident plants and animals will colonise the surrounding soil.

growing season. A grassland community is much more complex than this simplistic picture of butterflies and wildflowers suggests however, and if the opportunity arises it is well worth introducing whole turves from other meadows established on similar soils. Of course the very diverse swards are far too precious to be chopped up for this kind of use, but occasionally (in fact, all too often) floristically rich meadows are destroyed for one reason or another. Under these circumstances a turf-transplant is worthwhile, and turves introduced at random into an established but less interesting sward will often settle in quickly and contribute comprehensively to the wildlife community.

Creating meadows from seed

Creating a new wildflower meadow from seed on open soil is rather easier than diversifying established grassland – provided the ground preparation is good. The secret is still low fertility; it is best to avoid topsoil completely. A clean, low-nutrient subsoil is what is needed. A nutrient-rich soil will simply promote vigorous growth of a few species, and these will crowd out the rest.

Ideally, the soil should be spread in mid-summer, when there is less risk of machines compacting wet soil. In any event the final grade should be achieved before the end of the growing season. Cultivate to an even tilth and firm the surface to avoid subsequent settlement. There is no need to breakdown every lump of soil however. More seed seems to germinate if the surface is a little rough – 50 mm (2 ins) lumps as a maximum.

It is best to establish meadow from seed on well-drained, nutrient-poor sub-soil.

Rich soils are likely to promote vigorous growth of a few species of coarse grass and weeds.

If the soil contains any surface vegetable material it will probably also contain seeds. Some of these are likely to be undesirable species, which may create serious difficulties for meadow establishment. Dock *(Rumex obtusifolius)*, for instance, seems to have seed in most soils, and does very well in freshly cultivated soil. If the levelled seed bed can be allowed a month or so of growing time – say mid-August to mid-September, many of the 'weed' seeds will germinate; the new shoots can then be sprayed off with a contact herbicide and the subsequent establishment of meadow species will be much more successful

The best time for sowing a meadow is early autumn. Mid-September is ideal. The alternative is April, but many species will not germinate in the first year from a spring sowing. The cold winter months provide vital frost treatment which

If the soil contains 'weed' seed, cultivate in late summer, allow the weeds to germinate and then kill the seedlings with a non-selective contact herbicide.

25

breaks the dormancy built into the seed of species such as cowslip *(Primula veris)*. The proportion of seed germinating, therefore, will probably be much greater following an autumn sowing.

The choice of species is a matter of great debate. A meadow is a mixture of grasses and broad-leaved plants, and the seed mixture must contain both. Aggressive or very coarse species of grass must be avoided, so a mixture free from ryegrass *(Lolium perenne)* is essential. Generally a mixture of bents and fescue grasses *(Agrostis* and *Festuca* spp.) is best, with a small percentage of the more unusual meadow grasses such as meadow foxtail *(Alopecurus pratensis)*, smooth meadow grass *(Poa pratensis)*, timothy *(Phleum pratense)* and sweet vernal grass *(Anthoxanthum odoratum)* included for good measure. The seedhouses which specialise in native wildflower seed production (Appendix 1) all offer standard non-rye mixtures for meadow culture. On most poor soils a standard non-rye amenity mix will give good visual results. If the management is correct, the most appropriate species in the mix will do best in any case and additional grass species will gradually colonise later.

The meadow wildflower seeds are the second ingredient in the mix. These are mostly quite choosy as to soil, and so it is normal practice to include a wide range – perhaps 20 species, on the assumption that perhaps half of them will thrive. If a colourful summer display is required, one or two species are particularly easy and very showy, and these should always be included. Oxeye daisy *(Leucanthemum vulgare)* is one; meadow buttercup *(Ranunculus acris)* is another. The specialist seed firms have produced four or five selected mixtures to suit a range of specific site conditions: sandy, non-acid soils; loams and alluvial soils; clay soils, etc. Some have also refined the mixtures further, to provide either species which flower at a low-level (and generally in spring to early summer) or taller species which flower mainly in mid to late summer.

26

The sowing rate should be very low. Seedling overcrowding can be a serious problem if too many seeds are sown. The seeds of most of the meadow species are very small – many hundred to the gram – and generally a rate of between 0.2 and 0.5 grams of wildflower seed per square metre (2-5 kg per hectare), and 1-1.5 grams of grass seed per square metre (10-15 kg per hectare) is appropriate. On very large sites, particularly where wind exposure is a problem, it has been found helpful to include a nurse species which will germinate quickly and grow rapidly in the first spring. It is vital to use a nurse crop which is non-persistent. The choise is between the annual westerwolds ryegrass *(Lolium multiflorum* ssp. *westerwoldicum)* at a rate of two grams per square metre (20 kg per hectare) or a mixture of colourful cornfield annuals such as poppy *(Papaver rhoeas),* corn marigold *(Chrysanthemum segetum)* and white campion *(Silene alba).* Whichever annual nurse species are chosen, they must be mown at least once in mid to late summer to stop them shedding seed. Otherwise they may dominate the open structure of the first year sward, and restrict development of the true meadow species.

Sowing at such low rates is not easy. Even distribution is vital, and because the seed varies in size so much, it is important to make sure the seed is very thoroughly mixed. The big seeds may even migrate to the top of the bag during the time they are in transit. It is also helpful to use a 'carrier' to bulk up the seed. The best material seems to be fine sawdust, so long as it originates from untreated timber. A more expensive, heavier and therefore less convenient alternative is silver sand.

In both cases the increased bulk helps spread the seed more evenly, and the light colour makes it much easier to see where the seed is landing.

For small areas seed can be broadcast by hand. On larger areas a tractor-mounted fertilizer hopper is useful, and good results have also been achieved using a hand-operated lawn-fertilizer applicator, and even an old-fashioned seeding 'fiddle.'

*Sow very low rates of a mixture of wildflower
seed, fine meadow grasses, and a short-lived
nurse-crop – all bulked up with sawdust or
silver sand.*

Immediately after sowing it is helpful to scuffle
the surface lightly with a rake or a chain harrow.
Rolling with a light Cambridge roller helps firm
the seed bed. The nurse will often germinate
within a week to ten days in mild weather.
Autumn sown meadow species will mostly remain
dormant until the following spring.

One interesting alternative to seed sowing
which has produced spectacular results in Holland
and Sweden is the use of hay from species-rich
meadows. If the hay is cut and loose-baled when
it is still a little green, most of the seed will remain
attached to the seedheads. At the site of the
proposed new meadow, the hay is spread loosely
over the cultivated surface, and left to collapse
over the winter. The seed falls from the hay onto
the soil surface, and in the following spring it
germinates under the protection of the hay
covering. It seems that the lack of sunlight

*Spread a thin layer of fresh hay from a species-
rich meadow over the prepared seed bed.*

Clay soils meadow mix: % by weight

Wildflowers

Yarrow	*Achillea millefolium*	5.0%
Black knapweed	*Centaurea nigra*	5.0%
Meadow-sweet	*Filipendula ulmaria*	5.0%
Meadow cranebill	*Geranium pratense*	5.0%
Square stemmed St John's wort	*Hypericum tetrapterum*	5.0%
Oxeye daisy	*Leucanthemum vulgare*	15.0%
Ragged robin	*Lychnis flos-cuculi*	5.0%
Cowslip	*Primula veris*	5.0%
Self heal	*Prunella vulgaris*	5.0%
Yellow rattle	*Rhinanthus minor*	5.0%
		60.0%

Meadow grasses

Creeping bent	*Agrostis stolonifera*	5.0%
Meadow foxtail	*Alopecurus pratensis*	10.0%
Sweet vernal	*Anthoxanthum odoratum*	10.0%
Yorkshire fog	*Holcus lanatus*	5.0%
Meadow barley	*Hordeum secalinum*	5.0%
Golden oatgrass	*Trisetum flavescens*	5.0%
		40.0%

This mix to be mixed in a 1 to 2 ratio, with a commercial non-ryegrass seed mixture.

reaching the soil's surface prevents germination of annual 'weed' seed, but does not inhibit the meadow species. Obviously bales of species-rich hay are not an abundant commodity in the middle of towns, but this is a technique which could be extremely useful once the first seeded meadows or diversified swards are established. The hay from phase one could well provide a free means of establishment for phase two and beyond.

The hay sheds its wildflower and grass seed; germinating meadow-plant seedlings are protected whereas annual 'weeds of cultivation' are suppressed by the light mulch.

After sowing, bury the seeds lightly with a chain harrow or the back of a rake, and then firm gently with a Cambridge roller or with the feet.

Dry meadow mix: % by weight

Wildflowers

Yarrow	*Achillea millefolium*	1.0%
Hardheads	*Centaurium erythraea*	3.0%
Viper's bugloss	*Echium vulgare*	1.0%
Spotted hawkweed	*Hieracium maculatum*	3.0%
Slender St John's wort	*Hypericum pulchrum*	3.0%
Rough hawkbit	*Leontodon hipidus*	1.0%
Oxeye daisy	*Leucanthemum vulgare*	7.0%
Musk mallow	*Malva moschata*	2.0%
Vervain	*Verbena officinalis*	1.0%
		20.0%

Meadow grasses

Sweet vernal	*Anthoxanthum odoratum*	25.0%
Crested dogstail	*Cynosurus cristatus*	25.0%
Wavy hairgrass	*Deschampsia flexuosa*	20.0%
Yorkshire fog	*Holcus lanatus*	10.0%
		80.0%

This mix to be mixed in a 1 to 4 ratio with a non-rye commercial meadow mix, typically:

Browntop	*Agrostis tenuis*	10.0%
Dwarf creeping red fescue	*Festuca rubra* spp. *tutoralis*	15.0%
Normal creeping red fescue	*Festuca rubra* spp. *rubra*	35.0%
Hard fescue	*Festuca longifolia*	35.0%
Smooth stalked meadow grass	*Poa pratensis*	15.0%
		100.0%

First year establishment

By late May or early June, the meadow seedbed should be a carpet of green. In most circumstances there will be a mixture of grasses, and annual and perennial wildflowers. When the seedling sward is about 100 mm (4 ins) tall it must be cut. Rolling with a light roller should precede this mowing. This will help firm the little plants into the soil, and reduce the risk of mower-blades uprooting them. Cut either with a reciprocating blade such as an Allenscythe or with a wheeled rotary set at least 50 mm (2 ins) high and remove the clippings. If they are left they are likely to encourage fungal disease.

In the first season, cut the sward down to 50 mm (2 ins) each time it reaches 100 mm (4 ins), and by the end of the summer the grasses will be well tillered, forming a good mat of prostrate shoots. The wildflower seedlings of most species sown will be well established and easily identified. Do not expect a display of flower colour in the first season. It is much more important to establish good roots.

The seedling sward must be cut – perhaps four times in the first year. Cut down to 50mm (2ins) each time it reaches a height of 100mm (4ins).

If flower colour is important – perhaps to convince the sceptics – include the cornfield weeds in your seed mix, and allow for a four or five week break in mowing in late June and early July. The 'meadow' will produce a blaze of colour from the poppies and corn marigolds which will excite the most hardened traditionalist. However, within a season or two most of these 'weeds of cultivation' will be overwhelmed by meadow flowers.

Tall growing weeds such as dock, fat hen and thistle are best pulled out gently by hand. Alternatively the regrowth from cut stems can be treated with the gel-form of a systemic herbicide.

It is very important to avoid the use of chemicals once the meadow is sown. Fertilizers of any sort will favour the less desirable species, and use of pesticides and herbicides will defeat the whole object of the exercise. If there are one or two embarrassingly tall broadleaved plants towering above the seedlings, it is best to rely on the mowing to eradicate them. If that approach is unacceptable, either hand-pulling or cutting down followed by treatment of the remaining leaves with a gel-based non-selective systemic contact herbicide such as glyphosate (sold as Tumbleweed, Roundup or Spasor) will do a good job.

If the soil is poor enough, it should be possible to settle into a twice-a-year mowing regime by the second season. If fertility is high it may take several years of 'harvesting' to bring the fertility down.

Selected reading

Dony, J.G., Perring, F. and Rob, C.M. (1980) *English Names of Wild Flowers*. 2nd edition. Botanical Society of the British Isles. London.

Duffey, E. *et al.* (1974) *Grassland Ecology and Wildlife Management*. Chapman and Hall, London.

Gorer, R. (1978) *Growing Plants from Seed*. Faber and Faber, London.

Heydecker, W. (ed). (1973) *Seed Ecology*. Butterworths, London.

Kozlowski, T.T. (ed) (1972) *Seed Biology*. Academic Press, New York & London.

London Ecology Unit (Hare, A.D. ed.)(1988) *London's Meadows and Pastures*. Ecology Handbook 8.

Roberts, E.G. (ed) (1972) *Viability of Seeds*. Chapman and Hall, London.

Rothschild, M., and Farrell, C. (1983) *The Butterfly Gardener*. Michael Joseph/Rainbird, London.

Stevens, J. (1987) *The National Trust Book of Wild Flower Gardening*. Dorling Kindersley, London.

Wells, T., Bell, S. and Frost, A. (1981) *Creating attractive grasslands using native plant species*. Nature Conservancy Council, Shrewsbury.

A true wood contains several layers of vegetation as well as decaying matter.

Chapter 3
Woodlands

*Our ancient woodlands are irreplaceable, yet
at the moment we are destroying them at an
alarming rate. It is possible, however, to
create a wildlife community within twenty to
thirty years which looks, smells, feels and
sounds like real woodland. This chapter
describes a number of different ways in
which we can begin to establish the woodlands of the next century. We can plant into
established grassland, revegetate open-
ground, underplant tired old parkland trees,
or simply give nature's natural process of
colonisation a helping hand.*

There is great confusion between 'tree planting'
and development of 'woodland.' A wood is much
more than a few trees. We spend tens of millions
of pounds every year on tree planting, with little
prospects of any of this commitment and effort
ever leading to the creation of genuine new
woodland. Indeed a combination of poor handling
of plants, inappropriate planting technique and
often immediate abandonment lead to perhaps
70-30% death rate within the first ten years.

If we embark on a programme of woodland
husbandry, there is no doubt that we can create
the real thing. We could provide an urban habitat
for bluebells, violets and primroses, for purple
hairstreak and speckled wood butterflies, for
nuthatches, warblers and woodpeckers.

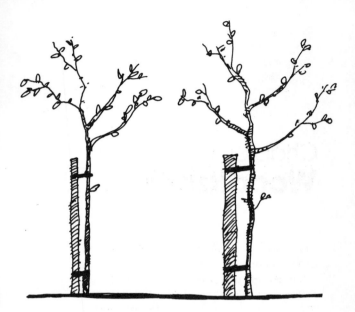

Nursery standard trees are rarely planted to form woodland.

Establishment of new woodland is effectively a commitment to a continued 'green' use for the land in question and a commitment to long-term creative management. Certainly a short-life scrub-community of broom or gorse, thorn or goat willow is a valuable habitat in its own right – and worth establishing on temporary sites earmarked for future development, road widening or some other anticipated use. True woodland, on the other hand, needs a great many years to mature. There is no shortage of suitable long-term land,

If grassland is simply left uncut it becomes

but it may well be worth securing a legally binding commitment to open space use before investing in a permanent woodland.

Public parks offer an immense opportunity for the creation of woodland, since they are already committed to open space use. Woodland is a marvellous recreational environment, and most parks have large areas of grass which are little-used. Development of a woodland belt around the park's perimeter will greatly improve shelter within. It will enhance the park's visual contribution to its neighbourhood, and it will reduce the financial commitment to grass cutting. Do try to make sure, though, that the new patch of woodland is not sited on the one area of grassland with real potential for meadow management. This has been a negative feature of so much field corner countryside tree planting in recent years.

Lessons from nature – letting a woodland develop 'naturally.'

Grassland is generally a temporary community, usually maintained by cropping of some kind. Take away the grazing livestock, the nibbling rabbits or the clattering mower blades, and in this part of the world the meadow will quickly develop into scrub. As the scrub matures, larger, longer-lived tree species will arrive, germinate under the protection of the often thorny shrubs and grow up to form a high woodland canopy. This process, known as natural succession, can be seen along stretches of previously mown motorway embankment all over the country. When mowing

a much richer habitat for wildlife.

Within a season or two 'pioneer' scrub species such

was stopped in the mid 1970s scrub species such
as hawthorn *(Crataegus monogyna)*, bramble
(Rubus fruticosus), blackthorn *(Prunus spinosa)*
and dog rose *(Rosa canina)* very quickly sprang
up. If there was oak nearby, jays delivered acorns,
buried them absentmindedly in the embankments,
and a colony of scrub-oak emerged. There are
now substantial saplings of ash, sycamore and
oak emerging from this scrub layer, and if mowing
is not renewed, there will be substantial blocks
of naturally regenerated woodland established
along the motorways by the end of the century.

Woodland planting schemes should aim
basically to give natural succession a helping
hand. With skill we can speed up the stages in
the process, and stretch out the more attractive
ones.

*Once established, the thorny scrub provides shelter
and protection, woodland tree species eventually grow*

as bramble, wild rose and hawthorn will invade.

Creating woodland in existing grassland
1 Scrub promotion

If we can learn to accept a little more untidiness (long grass and a tangle of stems – not bicycle frames, mattresses or polythene bags) the 'benign abandonment' approach has much to commend it. The scrub-habitat which precedes the development of a woodland structure is in itself extremely attractive to a wide range of animals. Typical species include songbirds such as the wren, blackbird and dunnock; butterflies including the skippers, meadow browns, gatekeepers and commas; small mammals such as the bank vole and the fieldmouse, and predators like the fox and the owl. This habitat is quick and easy to create.

through and over the shrubs.

In the establishment phase – say the first ten years – management will consist of two basic tasks. Firstly, the edges of the woodland development zone must be kept neat and tidy. A close-mown margin around the perimeter and along both sides of any footpaths which cross the area will give a clear indication that the wild area is intentional, and not simply a forgotten patch.

The second task in 'scrub-promotion' is to speed up the arrival of desirable plants. The typical pioneer species all have efficient adaptations for seed dispersal. Many grassland colonisers are transported by birds which typically feed on fruits of species such as blackberry, sloe, rosehips and haws in established scrub or hedgerow communities. They then roost in more open

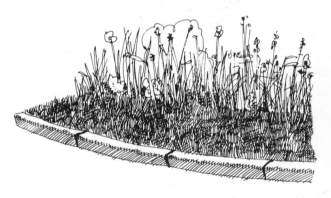

Developing scrub is accepted much more readily if the edges are kept looking neat and tidy.

grassland and there they excrete the seed. For plants with large seeds it is possible to simulate this dispersal process by introducing the seed artificially. Certainly this is an excellent way of establishing oak. The acorns are large-enough to handle easily, and a class of schoolchildren will take great delight in first collecting the nuts from nearby woodland, and then 'planting' them randomly across the site, simply by dropping them in the grass and pressing them down into the surface with their feet. The same technique works well with hazel nuts.

Large seeds such as acorn, blackthorn and hazel can be planted directly, simply by pressing them down into the soil.

2 Planting scrub species

Species with smaller seeds which come packaged in a soft edible fruit such as a rose-hip or a blackberry, are best established artificially as small individual plants. Apart from the physical difficulty of actually handling such small, sticky seeds, the process of bird-digestion does actually play a vital role in the natural colonisation process. The digestive juices in the birds' gut actually break down the seed's resistance to germination, and this stimulates seedling emergence in the first spring. A seed which is simply squeezed out of its fruit by hand may lie dormant for several years. Nurserymen have developed various techniques for breaking down natural dormancy artificially, using dilute acid, physical abrasion or severe frost treatment (all methods of stratification).

Two year old seedlings of native thorn-scrub species are extremely cheap to buy from nurserymen, and if planted in early autumn they are easy to establish. They are best planted randomly, but in groups of a single species – perhaps 25 in an area of 40-50 square metres. Success will be greatly improved if the seedlings are kept moist at all times and planted very firmly. Drench the roots immediately after planting. Success will be greatly improved if the seedlings are kept moist at all times and planted very firmly. In addition it helps if the top growth is cut back severely (to within 150 mm (6 ins) of the surface), and if an artificial mulch-mat of polythene or roofing felt is placed around the base of each plant.

New species should be introduced in simple random blocks. Avoid complex mixtures and straight lines.

This mulch helps to reduce competition for soil moisture from the grassland community within the first couple of seasons.

The young plants will almost certainly suffer some damage from rodents – particularly voles – in the first season or two, but this is rarely lethal and more often than not it simply stimulates vigorous suckering from the base.

Planting scrub species.

Keep the roots moist at all times

Plant firmly and cut the top growth back to within 150 mm (6 ins) of the surface.

Protect the seedlings against competition by using polythene or a roofing-felt mulch.

Woodland planting into soil

If a gradual 'scrub-development' approach is unacceptable or inappropriate, an instant community of young trees and shrubs can be planted into soil. However, under these circumstances it is vital to eliminate weed competition first. Ruderal plants such as dock *(Rumex obtusifolius)*, thistle *(Cirsium vulgare)*, fat hen *(Chenopodium album)* and couch grass *(Elymus repens)* are much more efficient at colonising and establishing themselves in cultivated ground than newly transplanted nursery-grown trees and shrubs.

If you are planting 'woodland' in an area of established vegetation, whether it is close-mown grass or a tangle of wasteland weeds, it is much better to eradicate the competition *before* planting than to try to eliminate it afterwards. Ideally the existing vegetation should be cut and raked off in mid-summer. Emergent regrowth should then be sprayed with a non-selective systemic contact herbicide in late summer. The area will subsequently be free of established perennial weeds in time for planting to be carried out in the autumn or winter months. There will still be an

Treat the regrowth with a contact herbicide before planting.

enormous reservoir of weed seed lying dormant in the soil, and the disturbance caused by planting will probably trigger off a mass germination of these seeds. However, this problem can be

44

prevented either by applying a residual pre-emergent herbicide (Simazine or Venzar) immediately after planting or preferably by covering the surface of the soil with a coarse mulch of chopped tree-bark. Fine granulated mulches such as peat, pulverized bark and mushroom compost are best avoided since they can aggravate

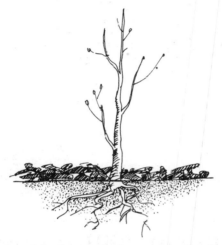

A mulch of coarsely chopped bark will prevent weed seeds germinating.

drought stress by absorbing moisture themselves; in addition they tend to become colonised by wind-blown surface-rooting weeds such as groundsel *(Senecio vulgaris)* and rosebay willowherb *(Chamerion angustifolium)* in the second season.

Trees planted into topsoil often die as a result of competition with vigorous weeds at their base. If soil is to be imported avoid topsoil at all costs. It is far easier, and much cheaper, to establish new woodland on sub-soil, or even crushed brick rubble, than it is to cope with the problem of weed growth from topsoil.

If the appropriate species of trees and shrubs are selected, it is possible to produce a five-metre high multi-canopied tree and shrub community on nutrient-poor demolition material within five

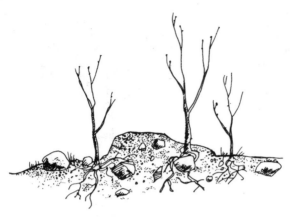

Planted woodland does best on nutrient-poor, weed-free soil.

years. Choice of stock, and techniques for planting are both critical to success. Elaborately staked standard trees are very expensive and a waste of time so far as potential woodland is concerned. Within two seasons a standard tree will usually be overtaken by a two-year old seedling which cost a fiftieth of the purchase price.

Plant large quantities of two-year old feathered seedlings. These are big enough to handle easily and yet small enough and adaptable enough to establish readily without elaborate staking etc. As with the scrub species, it is important to keep roots moist at all times. It is also worth dipping

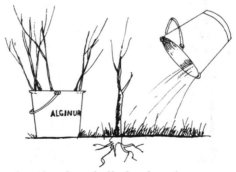

Drench with at least half a bucket of water per plant (4 litres) immediately after planting.

Plant 2 year old feathered seedlings.

the roots of the trees and shrubs in polyuronide root-dip (alginure) to increase moisture uptake in the first spring after planting.

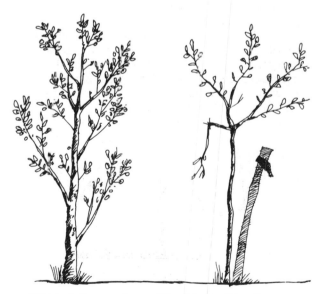

Within 2-3 years they will be bigger than the staked standards, and look much more natural.

Heavy pruning is also worthwhile. Shrub species can be chopped down to a stump of a few inches to stimulate bushy basal growth; tree species should have their side-shoots trimmed back in

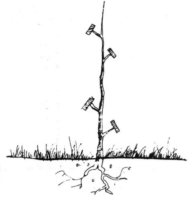

Trees:
Prune side shoots to promote upright growth.

Shrubs:
Cut hard back in late winter to promote bushiness.

order to promote sap-flow to the terminal bud, and hence more rapid vertical growth. Watering is essential at this growth stage. As a minimum, all plants should have their root-zone drenched with at least 4 litres of water immediately after planting. This settles the soil and dramatically improves survival. Periodic watering is unquestionably beneficial throughout the whole of the first summer, but it may of course be difficult to organize.

Choice of species is extremely important. There is a temptation to plant up a complete woodland all in one go. However, most of the true climax woodland species are unsuited to exposure and high light-levels, which is not surprising since they normally grow up in sheltered woodland. It is far better therefore to concentrate initially on pioneer species. The shrubs have already been described. They are the species found in pioneer scrub-communities. Some prefer high light levels, whilst others tolerate a range of light intensities. Begin by planting a continuous matrix of shrubs only. Forget about trees for the moment. Plant light-tolerant species in blocks of 10-25 over a 1 metre grid around the perimeter of your plantation. These might include broom *(Cytisus scoparius)*, gorse *(Ulex europaeus)*, blackthorn *(Prunus spinosa)*, dogwood *(Cornus sanguinea)*, guelder rose *(Viburnum opulus)*, field maple *(Acer campestre)* and the elder *(Sambucus nigra)*. In the centre of the plantation, plant pioneer species which will tolerate shade. These typically include hazel *(Corylus avellana)*, dog rose *(Rosa canina)*, bird cherry *(Prunus padus)*, wild privet *(Ligustrum vulgare)*, holly *(Ilex aquifolium)* and hawthorn *(Crataegus oxyacanthoides* and *C. monogyna)*. Bramble is another plant in the some category, but it is somewhat invasive, and is best left to find its

Light demanding edge shrubs planted at 1m centres in blocks of 10-25 of one species e.g. blackthorn, gorse, broom, field maple, dog rose.

Shade-tolerant 'undergrowth' shrubs planted at 1.5m centres in blocks of 10-25 of one species e.g. hazel, holly, wild privet, hawthorn, bird cherry.

First-stage tree species planted at 4-5m centres in extensive drifts of a single species. e.g. alder, birch, wild gean, whitebeam, ash.

Within the first season a two-layer structure will begin to develop.

own way into the mix. The shrubs should be grouped to form blocks of 10-25 of a single species. If they are cut back after planting, a dense closed canopy of undergrowth will be produced within three to four years.

Once the shrub layer is planted, a thin sprinkling of pioneer tree species should be introduced. On very poor, stony soil silver birch *(Betula pendula)* can do very well, whereas on soil with any degree of humus content better results will be achieved by planting pioneers such as alder *(Alnus glutinosa),* wild gean *(Prunus avium)* and ash *(Fraxinus excelsior).* If these tree species are planted in extensive drifts, at spacings of 4-5

After 10-15 years, the first-stage shrub canopy will grow over. Climax species can then be introduced.

metres, they will grow up through the shrub layer, and gradually extend to form an upper canopy. In ten to fifteen years there will be a comprehensive two layer woodland structure. Conditions will then be suitable for introducing longer-lived 'climax' tree species typical of the area – oak (*Quercus robur*), beech (*Fagus sylvatica*), hornbeam (*Carpinus betulus*) or lime (*Tilia* spp.)

Revitalizing existing stands of mature trees

Parks and formal gardens often have a legacy of over-mature trees standing in close-mown grass, some of which pre-date the current landscape. As these geriatric specimens decline, they present a wonderful opportunity for nature conservation and cry out to be revitalised as the basis of new woodland.

Stop mowing the grass. The shade and drought stress caused by the presence of the tree, which for years will have prevented healthy grass growth, will suddenly become an asset. There is unlikely

Shade and drought stress caused by the trees will generally prevent rampant grass and weed growth.

to be dramatic lush growth when cutting stops. Instead you may well see shade tolerant wildflowers begin to blossom. The ground beneath these trees should be underplanted with a mixture of shade tolerant woodland shrubs – the holly, hazel and bird cherry described above.

Underplant mature parkland trees with native shrubs and replacement tree seedlings.

Conditions are likely to be very hostile initially and it will be essential to water throughout the first two or three seasons. Make sure the new roots are drawn down by thorough soaking; inadequate wetting of the top layer of soil tends to encourage surface rooting. In the shelter of the mature tree canopy you can afford to plant direct replacements for the climax trees. If your mature species is beech, for instance, then plant more beech seedlings amongst the shrubs.

Replacement tree and shrub seedlings will need extra care with watering, particularly in the first summer.

Hedgerows

A mixed hedge is really a mini-version of the edge of woodland. We have lost thousands of miles of hedgerows since the war, and they are very valuable indeed as a habitat for wildlife. There is often evidence of old abandoned hedgelines in urban areas. These are well worth replanting, since reintroduction of the shrub layers will often result in colonisation by hedgerow wildflower species.

Plant a mixture of hedgerow shrubs at approximately 200 mm centres (5 per metre run) and plant in blocks of at least five of each species at a time. Look at existing old hedgerows in the area to see which species do well. A good 'average' mixture might include 60% hawthorn (*Crataegus* spp.), 20% field maple *(Acer campestre)*, 5% guelder rose *(Viburnum opulus)*, 5% dog rose *(Rosa canina)*, 5% holly *(Ilex aquifolium)* and 5% wild privet *(Ligustrum vulgare)*. It is best to avoid blackthorn *(Prunus spinosa)* since it tends to sucker and spread into adjacent grassland.

It is important to plant nursery stock grown from seed, and not from cuttings. This will give a more natural 'randomised' mix, and

Hedge seedlings should be planted at a rate of 5 per metre run. They should be protected against weed competition with a "hedgeline" mulch.

characteristics such as leaf and flower colour will also be varied.

Weed competition can be a problem in establishing hedgerows. A thin line of contact herbicide can be sprayed onto established swards before planting, though of course this will damage any wildflowers which may be there. Mulches are also useful, and in fact, a special 'hedgeline' mulch is available in polythene or felt, and can be purchased in 20 metre rolls.

Once the hedgerow is established it is advisable to cut it hard back, to stimulate bushy basal growth. After four or five years the hedgerow will be high enough to begin clipping annually; alternatively it can be layered every 7-10 years.

Tree seeding into open ground

It is possible to establish a colony of trees and shrubs by *seeding* directly into *open* soil. Here preparation to eliminate established weed growth is crucial since the seedling trees and shrubs are very vulnerable to competition. It is also impossible to control the development of new weed growth once the tree and shrub species have been sown. Any technique which controls the weed seedlings will also affect the trees.

The surface of the soil should be lightly cultivated to prepare the seedbed, and then rolled with a ridged (Cambridge) roller to produce a lightly corrugated surface. This is particularly important if the ground is sloping, and in this case the furrows must run across the slope. If they run up and down, rain will form gulleys and erode the soil. Allow time for weed seed to germinate and then kill seedlings with a contact herbicide.

Seed of suitable trees and shrubs is available commercially although it is always better to collect local indigenous seed wherever possible. An appropriate mixture would contain four or five pioneer shrub species and two or three tree species. The seed must be stored very carefully and best results will be achieved with an autumn sowing. Aim at a sowing rate which will deliver

15-20 seeds per square metre. Good results have been achieved by combining smaller seed with a nurse crop of winter wheat (at approximately 100 grains per square metre). Sow this combination first and then broadcast the larger seed of species such as oak, blackthorn and hazel separately. Follow the sowing with a light rolling, again with a Cambridge roller, to press the seed into the soil.

The winter wheat will germinate rapidly to produce a miniature forest of single stems. This will reduce the effect of drying winds and so improve the microclimate, whilst at the same time allowing plenty of light to reach the tree and shrub seedlings. This technique really must be restricted to very poor substrates otherwise weeds

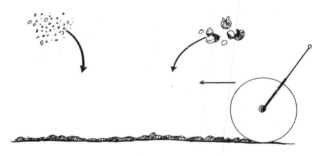

Sow fine seeds in a mixture with winter wheat (as a nurse). Hand sow larger seed separately. Firm with a Cambridge roller after sowing.

The winter wheat will grow up and provide shelter for the tree and shrub seedlings whilst suppressing weed seed germination.

will dominate. It is excellent for quarry waste, demolition rubble and gravel pit scars, and as might be expected, the species which respond best in these conditions are the birches and the willows – the pioneers of glacial moraine. The main weed problems will be sycamore and bramble; both may be controlled by spot-treatment with a contact herbicide, or weeded out by hand.

Diversifying the woodland for wildlife

Once the tree and shrub vegetation has established and forms a continuous dense canopy, it is possible to enrich the habitat in several ways.

A varied age structure is desirable and so some plants should be cut back each winter, to promote vigorous young growth. Climax trees should continue to be introduced if there is no sign of their arriving naturally.

Once the main structure is established, scrambling and climbing plants can be introduced. Bramble will almost certainly be there already. One species which will scramble happily and colourfully through the edge shrub layer is honeysuckle *(Lonicera periclymenum)*, a marvellous plant for evening perfume; it also attracts a great many nightflying insects and provides a colourful and valuable crop of winter berries. Another good choice is old man's beard *(Clematis vitalba)* – a rampant climber which is perhaps best held in reserve until the trees are quite substantial, otherwise they are likely to be overwhelmed.

A mulch of leaf litter or chopped bark helps woodland wildflowers to establish.

The herb, or wildflower layer of the woodland is difficult to establish. If the shrub canopy is opened up, this will trigger off germination of the old weed species of the original open space. The circumstances are quite different from those in old coppice woodland, where cutting results in explosion of woodland flowers rejoicing in the sunlight. It is necessary to lay down a woodland mulch. This can be either leaf-litter from other woods or parks, or shredded wood waste. Both materials are quite plentiful in many local authorities. The leaf-sweepings from the town squares and formal gardens are all too often burned and here is an excellent way of recycling them. Once thinning and coppicing begins within the planted areas, normally within ten years, the waste stems can be fed into a chipping machine, and returned to the woodland floor. In either event the mulch suppresses natural germination of the residual weed seed bank. Woodland wildflowers can successfully be planted through the mulch and in time they will colonise its surface. These can either be grown individually from seed, or introduced as turves from woodland elsewhere. The plants themselves are relatively easy to grow from seed, and as might be expected, they germinate best if given a leaf mould-based compost and light shading. Species to begin with could include foxglove *(Digitalis purpurea)*, primrose *(Primula vulgaris)*, white deadnettle *(Lamium album)*, red deadnettle *(Lamium purpureum)*, dog violet *(Viola riviniana)*,

Dead wood is an important part of the woodland habitat.

yellow archangel *(Lamium galeobdolon)*, red
campion *(Silene dioica)*, lesser celandine
(Ranunculus ficaria) and bluebell *(Endymion
non-scriptus)*. Of course snowdrops *(Galanthus
nivalis)* and wild daffodils *(Narcissus
pseudonarcissus)* are also very easily established
at the edge of new woodland.

Decay is vital for all wildlife communities, and is
particularly critical in woodland. In time natural
leaflitter will accumulate, trees and shrubs will die
and a natural cycle will develop, but that will take
very many years.

Importing the leaf-litter and wood-chip mulch
is an excellent way of boosting the habitat for
decay organisms. This can be enhanced further
by importing logs and even untreated construction
timbers, and leaving them to rot-down around the
woodland. Many of the wood-boring insects in

*Plantations can be diversified for wildlife by erecting nest
boxes, developing a ground flora, providing a modest*

particular have a winged stage in their lifecycle and can seek out new supplies of rotten wood. Of course if the odd branch or trunk is transported from an established wood into the new habitat, then along with the timber will come a ready-made community of creatures which can migrate to other rotting logs around the plantation.

A small pond in the 'woodland' will prove invaluable to wildlife. Ideally it should be permanently wet. It may be possible to drain surrounding slopes into a waterproof lined depression. (See Chapter 4). Alternatively, if the woodland forms part of a park or a school landscape the pond can be kept topped up with buckets of tap-water or a hosepipe.

Artificial nesting sites are a sophisticated way of enriching the habitat and boosting bird populations. Loose bundles of twigs, tied together and left in secluded corners will often provide nesting sites for wrens, robins and blackbirds. Open fronted nest boxes at various heights throughout the wood will attract spotted

water supply, introducing decaying wood and leaf litter, coppicing and planting shrubs, climbers and young trees.

flycatchers and again robins whilst a whole range
of small birds will take up residence in closed
nest-boxes if the hole-diameter is custom-built;
these include blue tits, great tits, tree-creepers,
starlings, woodpeckers and owls. The boxes
themselves should be very secure, difficult for
cats, magpies and other predators to reach and
they should be cleaned out every winter to avoid
a build up of parasites.

Commercial woodland

It is worth pointing out that urban woodland
could be revenue-earning. Whilst coniferous
softwood plantations are ecologically rather
unspectacular, the evergreen species, fir, spruce
and pines, certainly have a role to play. They are
particularly suited to exposed sites and thin soils.
Large blocks of such woodland would be far
preferable to acre upon acre of close-mown
rye-grass, and once an evergreen plantation
began to create a more sheltered local climate,
broadleafed woodland could be established in its
lea.

There is also a growing market for hardwood
coppice for firewood, fence posts and even paper-
pulp. Oak, hazel, wild gean, alder and many
other species all coppice readily. The process of
cutting down to the ground every ten to fifteen
years certainly adds interest and activity to the
urban landscape, as in Oxleas Wood in the
London Borough of Greenwich. Coppicing can
be a rewarding occupation and the value of this
management activity to wildlife is enormous.

*Hardwood coppice can be used for fenceposts and
footpaths in urban areas. This management activity is*

Selected reading

Beckett, K. and Beckett, G. (1979) *Planting Native Trees and Shrubs*. Jarrold, Norwich.

Brooks, A. (1980) *Woodlands*. BTCV, Doncaster.

Brooks, A. (1980) *Hedging*. BTCV, Doncaster.

Edlin, H.L. (1975) *Guide to Tree Planting*. 3rd edition. Collins, London.

Evans, J. (1984) *Broadleaved Silviculture*. Forestry Commission Bulletin 62. HMSO, London.

Jennings, T. (1978) *The World of a Hedge*. Faber and Faber, London.

Kennedy, C.E.J. and Southwood, T.R.E. (1984) The number of species of insects associated with British trees: a re-analysis. *Journal of Animal Ecology,* **53**, 455-478.

Mitchell, A. (1978) *A field guide to the Trees of Britain and Northern Europe*. 2nd edition. Collins, London.

Peterken, G. (1981) *Woodland conservation and management*. Chapman and Hall, London.

Southwood, T.R.E. (1961) The number of species of insect associated with various trees. *Journal of Animal Ecology,* **30**, 1-8.

Steele, R.C (1972) *Wildlife Conservation in Woodlands*. Forestry Commission Booklet 29. HMSO, London.

Stubbs, E.A. (1972) *Wildlife Conservation and Dead Wood*. Supplement to the Quarterly Journal of the Devon Trust for Nature Conservation.

Tregay, R. and Gustavsson, R. (1983) *Oakwood's new landscape. Designing for nature in the residential environment*. Warrington and Runcorn Development Corporation.

also extremely beneficial to the ground flora.

Chapter 4
Wetlands

Wet ground and open water provide a range of habitats for many highly specialised plant and animal species. Urban wetlands have become increasingly important as rural land drainage has resulted in the loss of much of our wetland heritage. However, it is worth noting that the Norfolk Broads, which are extremely rich in wildlife, are man-made ancient wetlands. We do have the technology to increase the wildlife value of ponds, lakes, gravel pits and reservoirs. This chapter describes techniques for improving the wildlife value of established wetlands and also gives guidelines on the creation of new ponds and marshy places from scratch.

Britain is internationally important for its wetland communities. Every autumn tens of thousands of ducks, geese, swans and waders fly here from the arctic regions of Scandinavia, Russia and Greenland. When they return north to breed the following spring, another massive migration of summer visitors flies north from Southern Africa. Both these groups of visitors are critically dependent on our wetlands.

In recent years, the number of large open water areas has probably actually increased. Gravel pits and reservoirs in particular have been

Wet grasslands and shallow water-margins are extremely rich in wildlife.

an inevitable side-effect of urbanisation. Deep water, then, is in relatively generous supply. It is the shallow ponds, the sluggish ditches, the wet meadows, reed beds and marshes which have been most severely depleted.

Improving existing open waters

Reservoirs, gravel pits and the more formal boating lakes and ornamental ponds all offer considerable opportunities for habitat creation. Relatively little wildlife is supported by a water depth of greater than two metres. By contrast water shallower than this can support a great diversity of plant and animal life. This is because light can penetrate shallow water areas; such areas also warm up comparatively quickly in the summer allowing much wildlife to thrive.

Creating shallow shelving margins is a first objective. If a wet gravel pit has been exhausted, or a concrete-edged park lake is no longer used for boating, tip in a quantity of clean material – preferably weedfree sub-soil, builders rubble and the like. Aim to provide a range of water depths, from almost nothing at all down to a metre or so. If the pond or lake bottom drops away suddenly beyond this depth, the spread of vegetation will be sharply contained and areas of uninterrupted openwater can be maintained easily.

Many of the aquatic animals are very territorial. This is particularly true of some of the shallow-water fish, wildfowl during the nesting season and a number of the more colourful insects. An indented and varied shoreline will certainly

An indented shoreline increases the range of wildlife territories.

Plant marginals into soft mud (preferably in April).

improve the habitat considerably by providing a number of easily defended territories.

Most marginal water plants are fairly specific about the depth of water in which they will grow. Along the very shallow margins, where the ground is marshy, some delightful wildflowers can be introduced. Yellow flag *(Iris pseudacorus),* flowering rush *(Butomus umbellatus),* marsh marigold *(Caltha palustris)* bur-reed *(Sparganium spp.),* greater spearwort *(Ranunculus lingua),* brooklime *(Veronica beccabunga)* and watermint *(Mentha aquatica)* all thrive with their roots in waterlogged mud or peat.

By the time the water depth has reached 150mm (6 ins) the marshy marginals tend to give way to another range of plants – the emergent species. These are able to grow up from the mud on the bottom, and send their flowers well above the water surface. Examples include water horsetail *(Equisetum fluviatile)* and water plantain *(Alisma plantago-aquatica).* However, if unchecked, reedmace *(Typha latifolia)* and the common reed *(Phragmites australis)* are likely to colonise much of the space at this depth.

Most of these water-edge plants are available commercially. Alternatively they can be introduced by transplanting from other ponds and lakes which have become overgrown. They are best moved in April/May once they have begun to shoot.

If the bottom of the pool or lake is soft, the roots of the aquatic plants can simply be pushed in by hand and held down by a stone. If the base is too solid for this, or if the water is inaccessible, it is possible to introduce the plants by tying the roots

For planting in deeper water tie soil and plant roots in a hessian bundle and toss gently into the water.

in a hessian or sacking bag together with some soil, and tossing them gently into the water. The weight of the soil causes the bag to sink and the roots and new shoots quickly grow through the material and colonise the adjacent lake floor.

The soil weighs the bundle down. Shoots and roots grow through the cloth and establish the plant.

Submerged aquatic plants are also important to the ecology of ponds and lakes. They provide both shelter and food for a wide range of aquatic animal life and they also play an oxygenating role. Bunches of plants of species such as water milfoil

(Myriophyllum spicatum), curled pondweed *(Potamogeton crispus),* and water starwort *(Callitriche stagnalis)* can again simply be weighted down with a stone or tied in hessian, and sunk in water up to two metres deep. There are also a number of attractive native plants which root on the bottom and produce floating leaves and flowers at the surface. Amphibious bistort *(Polygonum amphibium),* white water-lily *(Nymphaea alba),* yellow water-lily *(Nuphar lutea)* and water cowfoot *(Ranunculus aquatilis)* are all easy to establish. Other species, notably bogbean *(Menyanthes trifoliata),* will grow out from the margin across the water by floating stems.

On large or exposed areas of water, there may be considerable wave erosion on the windward shore. The wave action may disturb the new plants and prevent them from establishing. If this is a problem, some protection can be afforded by anchoring floating booms a metre or two beyond the edge of the planting. Lengths of buoyant timber, or long 'balloons' of inflated polythene tubing are both suitable but they must be firmly anchored to the bottom.

It should be pointed out that the nutrient status

submerged aquatics   *floating aquatics*

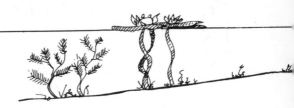

water milfoil   water lily
curled pondweed   amphibious bistort

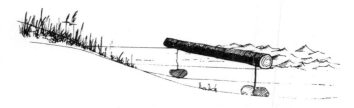

A floating boom firmly anchored to the bottom will protect the shoreline from wave erosion and encourage plant establishment.

of the water is as important as water depth in determining the species which will thrive in wetlands. Cotton grass *(Eriophorum angustifolium)*, for example, grows best in acid conditions, whereas water violet *(Hottonia palustris)* thrives in alkaline waters. Reedmace *(Typha latifolia)* can withstand domestic pollution.

New wetlands

New water bodies are easier to create now than they have ever been. Sophisticated and versatile machinery makes ground excavation relatively simple, and flexible sheet-liners have made water-proofing almost foolproof.

emergent plants   *marginal plants*   *marsh plants*

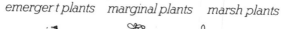

yellow flag   *ragged robin.*
bur-reed   *bugle.*
lesser spearwort   *meadow buttercup.*
brooklime   *marsh marigold.*
reed   *flowering rush*   *marsh orchid.*
reedmace   *water mint*

67

New ponds and lakes are most successful if
they can be constructed at natural watertable
level, either by damming a watercourse, or by
excavating down into its adjacent flood plain. If
any stream or river is to be dammed, it is vital to
obtain the approval of the drainage authority, and
the construction of all but the most modest of
damming structures must be designated by a
qualified structural engineer.

Off-stream ponds are much less complicated
to create, so long as the watertable does not
fluctuate dramatically. Recreational land is very
often located along river valleys, occupying areas
unsuited to building because of a high water-table

*New pools can be constructed by excavating
down to the water table.*

and the threat of flooding. Simply excavating into
the flat land beside the stream or river will create
water-bodies. Wet gravel pits demonstrate this
beautifully. If creating a new pool in this way,
excavate a shelving, indented shoreline and take
the water depth down to at least 1-1.5 metres to
ensure the retention of some open water.

It is very important to make *positive* use of the
spoil excavated from a new pond. If it is sand or
gravel there may be a chance of exploiting it
commercially, or at least using it for construction
purposes elsewhere in a habitat creation scheme.
Avoid the temptation to 'build landscape mounds'

new lake

A 200mm (8ins) layer of puddled clay will remain waterproof as long as it remains permanently covered with water. If it ever dries out it will crack and leak.

with it unless they can be designed to serve some positive purpose such as a visual screen for birdwatching, or physical protection for a seating area.

If the watertable fluctuates too much, or is simply too far down to be tapped, then of course pools, ponds and even huge reservoirs can be created and made waterproof by lining artificially.

Until recently, the only technique available for lining waterbodies of any size was clay puddling. Thousands of miles of contour canals were lined with puddled clay, and they are still remarkably sound a hundred or more years later.

If there is a ready supply of heavy clay of appropriate consistency, clay puddling is still well worth considering for pond lining. The technique is relatively simple. A continuous layer of clay, at least 200 mm (8 ins) thick, is spread across the bottom of the excavation and up the sides; it is kept watered, and then vigorously pummelled until it forms a continuous waterproof layer. Traditionally herds of cows were used to do the puddling – led in at one end of the canal and driven through. The modern alternative might be

stream

large groups of excited children in wellington boots. If it is to be puddled by rolling the clay needs to have some grit in it to hold together.

In most circumstances it will be cheaper, and certainly much more convenient to line ponds with a modern flexible sheet liner. There are several alternative materials available. Butyl rubber is the best. It can be pre-fabricated to any size and shape by vulcanising, either on site or at the factory, and it is extremely tough – virtually impossible to tear through, though rather more susceptible to puncturing. It is expected to last at least 50 years, and probably much longer. Terylene-strengthened plastic sheeting is not quite as expensive as butyl, but neither is it so long-lasting. It is easily punctured, though again very tear resistant. Polythene sheeting is a very popular flexible waterproof material, which, if used properly, can produce excellent results for about one third of the material cost of butyl. Use 1000 gauge black polythene as a minimum specification. It is very easily damaged and must be handled extremely carefully. Sheets can be joined successfully using a double-sided self-adhesive tape specially produced for the job.

Polythene deteriorates very rapidly in sunlight – even under several feet of water. The ultra-violet light makes the plastic brittle, and it splits. All construction using flexible liners must therefore

Use excavated material positively e.g. as a screen for birdwatchers.

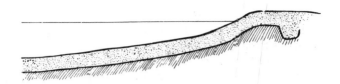

Extend the flexible liner beyond the edge of the pool. A gentle shelving margin is essential.

100mm (4ins) minimum covering of subsoil.

butyl liner ——→

protective layer of fibre matting or folded newspapers to prevent puncture by sharp stones.

include an over-layer of soil, sand, gravel or some other loose material. This cuts out the sunlight and protects against physical puncture. A layer of newspaper or other soft material below the liner also helps to prevent puncture from sharp stones, rubble etc.

Ponds should be sited on level ground, and if they are to look natural they should be low-lying. Water rarely collects on high ground or on the side of a hill. Try to arrange for rain-water from surrounding land to drain into the pond, or make provision to collect and pipe from adjacent roofs. Even car park run-off can be used so long as an oil trap is built into the system to prevent pollution of the pond. Rainwater (or streamwater) is always

preferable to tap water, though in times of drought it may be necessary to top up from a hose or fire-hydrant – with permission of course.

The provision of an overflow is just as important as a water-source. It may be practicable to arrange for surplus water to escape into a convenient storm-water culvert. Alternatively, particularly on well drained soils, an adequate soakaway should be excavated, and then backfilled with free draining gravel or clean brick rubble. Again, for large projects, professional advice should be sought.

Top up with natural drainage.
Provide for overflow into a storm-water culvert or a soakaway.

Wetland habitats should not be restricted to open water. Small marshes can be created artificially by extending the artificial waterproof lining beyond the margin of the new pond or lake, and backfilling with soil. Ideally, excavated material from established wetlands should be

Extend the pond to create a shelf of wet ground.
This will provide an excellent habitat for many wetland wildflowers.

used to form the marsh, since this will create an instant and comprehensive wildlife community. It is relatively easy too, since many wetlands rapidly silt up, and dredging is an important part of maintenance. Avoid using topsoil for marsh-building. It will be full of terrestrial or dry-land

Provide a range of vegetation types at the water's edge:

Close-cropped or mown grass is attractive to grazing ducks and geese (as well as picnickers).

Marginal and marshland vegetation is particularly good for wetland invertebrates.

Scrub gives valuable cover and safe access to the waterside for visiting wildlife.

Overhanging trees are attractive to look at and provide a safe roost for some species. However, shade restricts the growth of some water plants. Restrict trees to northern shores where possible.

weeds which can, nevertheless, be quite persistent and hinder the establishment of marshland plants. Weed free sub-soil will create a passable substitute, and can be used as an under-layer if only limited amounts of marshland soil are available. The essential ingredient for long-term success, however, is the consistently high watertable.

Plants should be established in new wetlands following the guidelines described for modifying existing wetlands.

Whilst the plant community can be built up quite rapidly, some invertebrate populations colonise new water bodies somewhat slowly. It is probably worth introducing some organic matter in the form of chopped straw to provide a mini-habitat for the larvae of several of the water insects. Experimental work on gravel pits managed by the Game Conservancy has yielded dramatic results, and a boom in small invertebrates such as chironymid larvae has a knock-on effect. It significantly improves the survival rate of many of the ducklings and predatory fish.

In newly excavated ponds and lakes, chopped straw spread on the surface in autumn will sink and form a valuable habitat for invertebrates.

Other aquatic animals are surprisingly mobile, and these will find and colonise new areas of open water very quickly. Aquatic insects such as wirlygig beetles, water boatmen, pondskaters and dragonflies will often arrive within a day or two of filling a new pond. Even flightless species such as leeches and watersnails are frequently transported on the legs of waterbirds or mixed with the tangle of water plants.

Some animal species can be introduced quite easily, though it is always best to ensure that the vegetation is well established first. The simple introduction of mud and leaf litter from the margin of a well-established species-rich pond, canal or lake will provide an excellent source of both larvae and eggs and will often contain viable seeds of aquatic plants too.

Transferring mud and leaf litter from a well established pond or canal is an effective way of introducing invertebrates such as damsel fly and diving beetle larvae, as well as the seed of water plants.

Undisturbed sanctuary areas are particularly important to wetland wildlife. The vegetation is very easy to damage by trampling, and many of the animals are particularly timid. The open

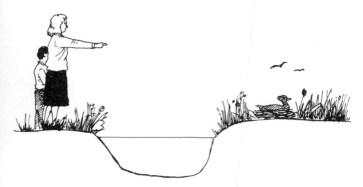

Water can be used to restrict access to sensitive areas.

nature of the habitat tends to make it difficult to approach wetland birds, for instance, without frightening them away.

The water itself can be used as a barrier to access. If ditches are incorporated into a scheme, for example, these can be designed to be permanently wet, and made too wide to jump across.

In open water it is well worth providing at least one island. If the pool is artificial and the water no more than a couple of metres deep, an island can be built from the floor of the pool by re-using some of the excavated material placed back on top of the pool liner. A water body excavated into

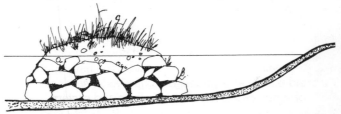

Islands are best constructed on top of the liner in artificial pools.

the natural watertable can be left with islands which are simply bits kept unextracted. Make sure that the island shore is too far from the

Aquatic plants can be established in wire baskets below the raft.

In deep water, floating raft-islands should be planted with wetland plants and anchored firmly in position using steel hawsers.

The ideal wildlife island will have a gently sloping 'basking beach' facing south and a tangle of bramble scrub to the north.

waterside for foxes (or people) to jump across the gap. In deep water floating island-rafts firmly anchored to the bottom, can provide an excellent sanctuary for both roosting and nesting birds.

Ideally, a wildlife island should again have an indented shoreline. It should have a dense tangle of scrub-vegetation on its northern and eastern sides, and an open beach of shingle or gravel on its southern edge. On all sides the island should slope gently down into the water.

Gently shelving edges allow animals to get in and out of the water easily

Planting bramble and wild rose will produce the kind of thorny tangled nesting habitat which is

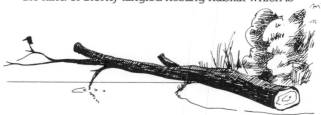

A dead tree or large branch running out into the water provides an excellent bird roost and a fishing perch for kingfishers.

The basking beach can be kept free of vegetation by spreading gravel over an impervious layer of polythene.

particularly popular with mallard and other ducks. A dead branch or two extending out into the water will provide a safe roost for ducks, and may well become a popular fishing perch for kingfishers. An open basking beach can be contrived by laying down an impenetrable barrier of polythene at the waters edge immediately below a layer of 100 mm (4 ins) of soil-free gravel. This will stay free of weed growth for several seasons (an important consideration when access for management may be rather inconvenient), and ducks will congregate there in safety, to bask. The basking shore must be very gently sloping indeed. The lack of vegetation cover makes it especially vulnerable to erosion, and the southern shoreline is often the one most exposed to wave action stimulated by prevailing south-westerly winds.

Another tactic for reducing disturbance is that of providing very positively for restricted public access. Observation hides, footbridges and walkways all help increase access to wildlife, whilst at the same time minimise disturbance.

Hopefully, by making urban wetlands more attractive, we shall avoid the long tradition of dumping old bicycles, prams, mattresses, etc into our ponds, canals and lakes. Perhaps reed-fringed ponds with water lillies will be more appreciated and not simply regarded as dumping grounds.

Wetland management

A wet meadow community must generally be cropped once a year if it is to remain free from willow and alder scrub. Ideally grazing animals should be used, and for preference, stock-cattle. Late summer and autumn grazing will take off the summer growth, and have the added benefit of poaching or churning up the wetter areas. Poaching is particularly valuable to wildlife. It creates gaps in the plant cover in which new seedlings can establish and it provides small puddles which are excellent sites for many invertebrates.

Grazing is a possibility on some urban sites, with the growth of city farms and the increasing popularity of horse riding. It is important not to over-graze. The aim should be to take off the taller

Tipping leads to pollution. Prevent vehicle access to the water's edge where possible. Remove rubbish immediately.

growth and not to erode the sward. Sheep are generally unsuitable, partly because they are vulnerable, in urban areas, particularly to dog worrying, but also because they suffer from several diseases which are encouraged by wet conditions. In addition, they tend to graze too closely for many of the more interesting wetland wildflowers to survive.

If grazing is out of the question, mowing of wet ground obviously presents a considerable problem. One simple solution adopted in some artificial wet meadows in Holland, is to wait until the hard winter frost freezes the wetland surface, and then cut the vegetation down. Removal of the cuttings is less important in wet meadows than in dryer meadows, because most of the coarse grasses are inhibited by the water-logged conditions and the more colourful wetland wildflowers are able to compete. It is, therefore, acceptable simply to cut and leave the 'harvest'. On small areas the vegetation above the frozen surface can be cut by hand using a scythe. Alternatively, a wheeled or an air-cushioned machine can be used. It is probably too risky to use heavy ride-on machines in most parts of Britain, unless the weather is quite exceptionally cold.

Where the ground is wet but firm underneath – as would be the case on a rubble-filled site with a high watertable and a thin covering of soil,

Wet meadows can be grazed by cattle.

Alternatively cut with a mower when the ground is frozen…

…or 'scythe' using a strimmer.

excellent results can be achieved by walking over the meadow with a 'strimmer.' This is a hand operated machine which cuts grass and other herbage using a fast-revolving length of nylon cord or wire. The whiplash action is very effective and this machine is perhaps the modern equivalent of the scythe. Many parks departments now employ strimmers for cutting grass against walls, lamp posts and other awkward vertical obstacles.

Natural wetland vegetation tends to change gradually because of the build up of peat, or silt. This accumulation may raise the ground level. As the water becomes shallower as a result, the wetland plants are replaced by more and more dryland species. It may be appropriate to simply allow this progression to happen, and enjoy the change. This may follow a pattern whereby open water is colonised by emergent reed bed or marshland communities. The marsh may develop into a wet alder or willow woodland before reaching the climax – normally oak.

Once established, willow and alder scrub is difficult to eradicate and active removal may be the only means of maintaining wetland vegetation. If the process of silting and the resulting habitat change is to be avoided, or at least slowed down, it is important to stop the silt building up. Where the wetland is fed by a stream or ditch, it is relatively easy to install a silt-trap at the entrance to the site. Direct the flow over a shallow tank set into the streambed. As long as the rate of flow is slowed down the silt will precipitate out. On a small scale the tank can be designed for emptying by hand with a bucket and shovel. On a larger scale it will be worth allowing for tractor and trailer access; a tractor bucket can then be used to scrape out the silt.

Selected reading

Brooks, A. (1981) *Waterways and Wetlands*. 2nd edition. BTCV, Doncaster.

Department of Environment, Ministry of Agriculture, Fisheries and Food, Welsh Office Agriculture Department (1982) *Land drainage and conservation*: guidance notes on procedures for Water Authorities, Internal Drainage Boards, Nature Conservancy Council and Countryside Commission. Section 22 of the *Water Act 1973* as amended by Section 48 of the *Wildlife and Countryside Act* 1981. HMSO, London.

Game Conservancy (1981) *Wildfowl Management on Inland Waters*. Booklet No. 3. Fordingbridge.

Harrison, J.G. (1976) *Wetlands for waterfowl*. Council of Europe, Strasbourg.

Jeffries, M. and Mills, D.H. (1990) *Freshwater Ecology: Principles and Applications*. Belhaven Press, London.

Lewis, G. and Williams, G. (1984) *Rivers and Wildlife Handbook: A guide to practices which further the conservation of wildlife on rivers.* Royal Society for the Protection of Birds and Royal Society for Nature conservation.

Macan, T.T. (1973) *Ponds and Lakes.* Allen and Unwin, London.

Macan, T.T. and Worthington, E.B. (1974) *Life in Lakes and Rivers.* 3rd edition. (New Naturalist Series.) Collins, London.

McCoy, P. (1986) *Water Gardening.* Blandford Press, Poole.

Newbold, C., Purseglove, J. and Holmes, N. 1983 *Nature Conservation and River Engineering.* Nature Conservancy Council, Peterborough.

Water Space Amenity Commission (1980) *Conservation and Land Drainage Guidelines.* London.

Witton, B.A. (1979) *Rivers, Lakes and Marshes.* (The natural history of Britain and Northern Europe Series.) Hodder and Stoughton, London.

Chapter 5
Wastelands

Some wildlife is extremely adaptable. Many vacant or 'gap' sites and other areas of urban disturbance can provide a colourful and fascinating dynamic habitat. They can also offer great scope for environmental education and for adventurous play. This chapter offers suggestions for making wasteland more socially acceptable, and for increasing its ecological richness.

There is a vast acreage of land in every conurbation which is described rather unkindly as derelict, or wasteland. A better description might be 'disturbed land' and certainly in ecological terms that is its essential characteristic. Mining, quarrying, industrial building, tipping, railway and road construction; these and many other urban activities have devastated huge areas of land, and left them to recover as best they can. Some of the older dereliction has recovered. These areas are now extremely valuable as

Many wastelands are dynamic communities of coarse ruderal weeds including thistle, dock and willowherb, garden escapes such as golden rod and buddleja, and highly mobile opportunist wildlife including seed-eating finches, nectar-feeding butterflies and scavenging foxes.

established and relatively stable communities, and deserve positive management as orthodox woodland, wetland or meadow. The more recent dereliction – particularly that resulting from demolition, represents an enormous area of land which supports a more dynamic wildlife. It is a community of familiar ruderal weeds – typically thistles, docks, willowherbs, groundsel, and in fact it supports an enormous variety of highly adaptable and mobile animal life too. This is the typical landscape of gap sites. Often is is enriched by a number of non-native plants. These exotic species have their origins in gardens and allotments and include spectacular flowers such as the butterfly bush *(Buddleja daviddi)*, goldenrod *(Solidago canadensis)*, and michaelmas daisy *(Aster* ssp.) as well as the extremely invasive Japanese knotweed *(Polygonum cuspidatum)*.

The landscape often provides the first adventure playspace for city children. This is the vegetation for cowboys and indians, for den-building and for BMX trails.

Wasteland sites are often in private ownership. They frequently have 'hope value' in the eyes of developers and are therefore, not usually available

Restricted vehicular access, proper signposting and a neat, tidy margin will all help give wasteland communities a more respectable image.

for long-term habitat creation. However, they can be immensely valuable in the short-term as an education resource and as a temporary stop-over point for wildlife.

The diversity and interest of wasteland sites can be increased by careful management. Firstly, the image must be one of intentional, respectable wildness. This is best effected by keeping the edges, particularly the road-frontages, tidy. Fly tipping can often be stopped by making vehicular access impossible and it is certainly worth labelling the site. It is quite amazing how readily people will accept wild places if they are given a name. If the signboard can explain something of the wildlife community, so much the better. Active educational use also helps change the image of "just an old demolition site covered in weeds." The William Curtis Ecological Park by Tower Bridge in London was a spectacular example of an invasive weed community made respectable through appropriate interpretation (see also Chapter 6).

The second key to successful wasteland management is ground disturbance. Essentially the plants are annuals, biennials or short-lived perennials. They typically have very bright flower colours and produce masses of windblown seed. They need open soil if they are to continue from generation to generation, and that means disturbing the ground. On a large, relatively level site it may be possible to 'scuffle' the surface during the winter using a tractor and spiked harrow. If the site is too small or too cluttered with rubble and junk, merely 'roughing up' the surface here and there with a garden fork or a steel rake each year will maintain the plant community.

The process of disturbance also provides a good opportunity to increase the range of plants by scattering seed. Poppies, corn marigolds, corn cockle and chicory are native plants which grow well in these areas. Some of the colourful non-natives do well too. For instance, most of the popular garden annuals, such as Californian poppy, night-scented stock, virginia stock and candytuft, thrive on wastelands, as do some of the more aggressive biennials and perennials including evening primrose, mallow and red-hot poker. The flowers attract a wide range of insects and are usually extremely good for butterflies and moths. Wasteland plants also provide a vital food source in winter for seed-eating birds. The finches in particular, feed in flocks on the seed of teasels, thistles, mulleins, docks and many other 'weeds.'

Flocks of finches feed on the seed and colourful insects feed on the nectar of wasteland plants.

Selected reading

Civic Trust (1977) *Urban Wasteland: a report of land lying dormant in cities, towns and villages in Britain.* London.

Cole, L. (1980) *Wildlife in the City: a study of practical conservation projects.* Nature Conservancy Council, Peterborough.

Denis, E. (1972) *Everyman's Nature Reserve: ideas for action.* David and Charles, Newton Abbot.

(continued over)

Selected Reading (cont.)

Ecological Parks Trust. (1978) *The William Curtis Ecological Park: first report 1977-78.* London.

Gemmell, R.P. (1977) *Colonization of industrial wasteland.* Studies in Biology No. 80. Arnold, London.

Gilbert, O.L. (1983) The Wildlife of Britain's Wasteland. *New Scientist, 97,*824-829.

Greater London Council, (1986) *A Nature Conservation Strategy for London: Woodland, Wasteland, the Tidal Thames and two London Boroughs.* Ecology Handbook 4. London Ecology Unit, London.

Lavender, S. (1981) *New Land for Old: the environmental renaissance of the lower Swansea Valley.* Adam Hilger. Bristol.

Stearn, J. (1981) *Towards community uses for wasteland.* Wasteland Forum. London.

Chapter 6
Interpretation and Education

*The success of habitat creation schemes
does not only depend on ecological
techniques. It is also necessary to explain
to people the value of attracting wildlife to
towns and cities. Wardens or interpreters
could draw attention to the need to create
habitats and the vast opportunities which
exist.*

Telling people what is going on

People in towns have become used to a neat and
tidy environment. The subtle attractiveness of
wildflower meadows, scrub-woodland and
lakeside reed beds will naturally take a little
getting used to. It is very important, therefore, to
explain what is happening. A simple notice which
makes the new landscape 'official' will satisfy
many of the potential critics. However, there will
be times of the year, and stages in development,
when the landscapes really does look rather
scruffy. This is why it is important to explain the
ecological basis of wildlife communities. Probably
the best way of developing public enthusiasm
and gaining support is to capitalise on the
established public love of certain 'spectacular'
types of wildlife. Take butterflies, for example.
Most people find them beautiful. If we provide
illustrations in our parks, which help people
distinguish between small tortoiseshell and red
admiral, or between orange-tip and small white,
their enjoyment of the creatures themselves will
be increased. We can then seize the opportunity
to link these beautiful adults to their less popular
caterpillars, show people the vital food plants, and
explain that they are an essential part of the
habitat. It may subsequently become easier to
justify the patch of nettles in the corner of the

playing field (caterpillar food plant for red admirals, peacocks and small tortoiseshell) or the milkmaids *(Cardamine pratensis)* flowering their pretty pink heads off in the damper parts of the meadow (milkmaids are the larval food plant of orange-tip and many other butterflies).

Similarly, the way to convince people of the value of rough grass land, particularly in the winter months, is by celebrating the life-style of the kestrel. This beautiful hunter hovers above areas of long grass throughout the year, watching for the slightest movement in the tangle of leaves and stems which will betray the presence of a secretive bank vole, mouse or other prey species. The beautiful song of the skylark is another perfect advertisement for meadow-length grass. No meadows – no skylarks.

Signboards and leaflets are certainly better than nothing, but they are both rather limited. By far the best way of enthusing people about wildlife is by providing our open spaces with human interpreters. More and more local authorities are recognising the value of employing wardens or rangers who can work in the landscape, and help encourage visitors to enjoy the beauty of nature. The work of rangers can be usefully complemented by volunteers.

Traditionally, school grounds have been areas of close-mown grass and tarmac. Using the guidelines contained in this book we can create grasslands, woodlands, hedges and ponds to help in the teaching of environmental studies and enhance the school environment for all who work in it.

Habitat creation in schools

By creating wildlife habitats in school grounds children can come into intimate contact with nature and can learn to appreciate changes in the seasons, relationships between living organisms and their environment and the complexity of the whole food web. Indeed, wildlife habitats are excellent for teaching all subjects from art to maths. Close contact between children and plants and animals is likely to lead to a desire to conserve nature, not only in their own areas, but in the country side and wherever they go.

Nature sites in school grounds, being so accessible, allow teachers and children to visit sites regularly, at much less expense than an out-of-town field trip. If nature studies are fitted into the formal curriculum, children and indeed students of all ages, can gradually learn about, and become familiar with, the natural environment.

It is of course important that any new habitats created do not interfere with the efficiency of playing-field maintenance or create new problems for the caretaker. Any of the habitats described here *could* be created in school grounds; some, however, are particularly suitable. As we have seen, grasslands can be created by simply altering the mowing pattern. Alternatively, a small area could be used to create a meadow with a seed mix. Trees grown from seed by the children themselves can be planted into either a small copse or even a formal hedge. Even simpler is to cordon off an area which is just left to go wild. This makes a fascinating class exercise because the children can record what appears as the grassland gradually gets invaded by scrub and so on. Last but not least, the making of a pond is always a favourite; it is interesting to watch for pond life to appear seemingly all by itself in these self-contained ecosystems. Alternatively, as we have seen, animals can be introduced.

Of course the local authority must be consulted before any work is done. Also remember that any habitat created must be managed. The education authority may be able to help here, especially with the use of tools which can be dangerous, such as mowers for the grassland or shears in the woodland. Other tasks can and should be carried out as class or lunchtime activities. Tossing hay into the air, cleaning out excess algae from the pond or weeding the new woodland, are all tasks children may enjoy, and·

which contribute to the learning process.
Teachers and parents can help co-ordinate
management by forming parent/teacher groups
to look after the wildlife garden. The local Wildlife
Trust and/or Watch group can assist too (write to
Watch, RSNC, The Green, Nettleham, Lincoln,
LN2 2NR).

Older children can be involved in the writing
of explanatory leaflets and even nature trails to
explain the new school habitats. Imaginative use
of school grounds for wildlife habitats will allow
generations of children to learn valuable lessons
about the natural world.

General Bibliography

Angel, H. (1976) *Wild Animals in the Garden*.
Jarrold, Norwich.

Baines, J.C. (1985) *How to Make a Wildlife Garden*.
Elm Tree Books, London.

Baines, J.C. (1982) Urban Wildlife Conservation
and Recreation. *Natural World Magazine*.
RSNC, Lincoln.

Baines, J.C. (1984) *The RSPB Book of Nature
Conservation*. Sandy, Bedfordshire.

Barrington, R. (1971) *The Bird Gardener's Book*.
Wolfe, London.

Bradshaw, A.D. and Chadwick, M.J. (1980) *The
Restoration of Land*. Studies in Ecology; Vol. 6.
Blackwell Scientific Publications, Oxford.

Bradshaw, A.D., Goode, D.A. & Thorp, E. (Editors)
(1986) *Ecology and Design in Landscape*. 24th
Symposium of the British Ecology Society.
Blackwell Scientific Publications, Oxford.

Brooker, R. and Corder,M. (1986) *Environmental
Economy*. E. and F.N. Spon, London.

Brown, J. (1982) *The Everywhere landscape*.
Wildwood House, London.

Buckley, G.P., (Editor.) (1989) *Habitat
Reconstruction*. Proceedings of a conference

held at Wye College, April 1988. Belhaven
Press, London.

Chinery, M. (1977) *The Natural History of the
Garden*. Collins, London.

Clapham, A.R. Tutin, T.G. and Warburg, E.F.
(1981) *Excursion flora of the British Isles*.
Cambridge University Press.

Corder, M. and Brooker, R. (1981) *Natural
Economy: an Ecological Approach to Planting
and Management Techniques in Urban Areas*.
Kirkless Metropolitan Council, Huddersfield.

Council of Europe. (1982) *Nature in Cities*. Nature
and Environment Series No 28. Council of
Europe, Strasbourg.

Dawe, G.F.M. (1991) *An Introduction to Habitat
Creation*. Packard, Chichester.

Ecological Parks Trust (1982) *New Life for Old
Space: a guide to handbooks and leaflets
covering the principles and methods of
converting small urban sites into nature areas
in Britain*. EPT in association with NCC.

Emery, M. (1986) *Promoting Nature in Cities and
Towns*. Ecological Parks Trust. Croom Helm,
London.

Fairbrother, N. (1972) *New Lives, New
Landscapes*. Penguin, Harmondsworth.

Fitter, R.S.R. (1945) *London's Natural History*.
(New Naturalist Series). Collins, London.

Fitter, R.S.R. (1949) *London's Birds*. (New
Naturalist Series). Collins, London.

Grime, J.P. (1979) *Plant Strategies and Vegetation
Processes*. John Wiley, Chichester.

Kilpatrick, C. (1976) Wildlife in Towns. Almark,
London.

Laurie, I.C. (ed) (1979) *Nature in Cities*. Wiley,
Chichester.

London Wildlife Trust. (1985) *Encouraging
Wildlife in Urban Parks – Guidelines to
Management*. Gordon Press, London.

Mabey, R. (1973) *The Unofficial Countryside*.
Collins London.

Mabey, R. (1980) *The Common Ground*.
Hutchinson, London.

Ministry of Agriculture (1983) *Agricultural
Chemicals Approvals Scheme*. HMSO, London.

Mostyn, B. (1979) *Personal benefits and satisfactions derived from participation in urban wildlife projects: a qualitative evaluation.* Nature Conservancy Council, Peterborough.

Nature Conservancy Council. (1981) *Wildlife in the City.* Bibliography series No. 2. NCC, Peterborough.

Newman, L.H. (1967) *Create a Butterfly Garden.* John Baker, London.

Owen, D. (1978) *Towns and Gardens.* (The natural history of Britain and northern Europe series). Hodder and Stoughton, London.

Perring, F.H. and Farrell, L. (1982) *British Red Data Book: I. Vascular Plants.* 2nd edition. Royal Society for Nature Conservation, Lincoln.

Perring, F.H. and Walters, S.M. (eds). (1983) *Atlas of the British Flora.* 3rd edition. Botanical Society of the British Isles. London.

Royal Society for the Protection of Birds (1982) *Gardening with Wildlife.* RSPB, Sandy, Bedfordshire.

Ruff, A. (1987) Holland and the Ecological Landscapes 1973-1987. An appraisal of recent developments in layout and management of urban open space in the low countries. In: *Urban and Regional Studies,* 1, (Edited by T. Deelstra). Delft University Press, Delft.

Shoard, M. (1980) *The Theft of the Countryside.* Temple Smith. London.

Simms, E. (1975) *Birds of Town and Suburb.* Collins, London.

Smart, P.J. (1989) Common sense approaches to the construction of species-rich vegetation in urban areas. In G.P. Buckley, cited above.

Teagle, W.G. (1978) *The Endless Village. The wildlife of Birmingham, Dudley, Sandwell, Walsall and Wolverhampton.* Nature Conservancy Council, Peterborough.

Urban Wildlife Group. (1984) *Nature by Design. A Teacher's Guide to Practical Nature Conservation.* Educational Unit of the Urban Wildlife Group, Birmingham.

Urban Wildlife Group (1983) *Planning with Nature. A guide for all who help shape the environment of our towns.* Birmingham.

Appendix 1

**Specialist firms selling wildflower seed
originating from native British sources
(collected directly from the wild or harvested
from plants grown from such seed).
Please enclose a stamped addressed envelope
when writing to any of these addresses.**

John Chambers
15 Westleigh Road
Barton Seagrave
Kettering
Northamptonshire, NN15 5AJ
Tel· 0933-681632
Packeted seed and conservation mixtures;
seed by weight; plants and bulbs.

Emorsgate Seeds
Emorsgate
Terrington St-Clement
Kings Lynn
Norfolk, PE34 4NY
Tel: 0533-829028
Seeds and conservation mixtures by weight.

W W Johnson & Sons Ltd,
London Road
Boston
Lincolnshire, PE21 8AD
Tel: 0205-65051
Trade conservation mixtures and packets
available in garden centres.

Naturescape
Whatton-in-the-Vale
Nottingham
Nottinghamshire, NG13 9EP
Tel: 0949-51045
Packeted seed and conservation mixtures; plants

(continued over)

The Seed Bank
Cowcombe Farm
Gipsy Lane
Stroud
Gloucestershire, GL6 8HP
Packeted seed; seed exchange.

Suffolk Herbs Ltd.
Sawyer's Farm
Little Cornard
Sudbury
Suffolk, CO10 0NY
Tel: 0787-227247
Packeted seed and conservation mixtures;
seed by weight; plants.

Appendix 2

**Insects associated with the commoner
British trees. After Southwood (1961).**

Native trees	Associated insect species
Oak	284
Birch	229
Hazel	73
Willow	266
Alder	90
Hawthorn	149
Ash	41
Pine	91
Holly	7
Yew	1
Sloe	109
Poplars	97
Elm	82
Beech	64
Common maple	26
Hornbeam	28
Juniper	20
Lime	31
Mountain ash	28

Introduced trees

Sweet chestnut	5
Walnut	3
Holm oak	2
Larch	17
Sycamore	15
Horse chestnut	4
Acacia	1
Plane	0

NOTE: Although, on the whole, introduced species support fewer numbers of insects than native species, they do have many other advantages in habitat creation schemes. Sycamore, for instance, supports a large biomass of aphids (food for birds and other animals); other species provide a useful additional nectar source and many are attractive and often have their own local and cultural significance. In some parts of cities species like sycamore and buddleia are the only ones which will grow.

Appendix 3

Plant species suitable for establishment in grasslands, woodlands, wetlands and wastelands.

It is important to determine which species are suitable for particular localities so that natural geographical distribution patterns are maintained.

1. Grasslands

Botanical name	*Common name*
Achillea millefolium	Yarrow
Agrostis stolonifera	Creeping bent
A. tenuis	Browntop
Ajuga reptans	Bugle
Alopecurus pratensis	Meadow foxtail
Anthoxanthum odoratum	Sweet vernal
Anthyllis vulneraria	Kidney vetch
Bellis perennis	Daisy
Centaurea scabiosa	Greater knapweed
C. nigra	Hardheads or black knapweed
Centaurium erythraea	Common century
Chrysanthemum segetum	Corn marigold
Cynoglossum officinale	Houndstongue
Cynosurus cristatus	Crested dogstail
Deschampsia flexuosa	Wavy hairgrass
Echium vulgare	Viper's bugloss
Erigeron acer	Blue fleabane
Festuca longifolia	Hard fescue
F. rubra	Red fescue
Filipendula ulmaria	Meadowsweet
Geranium pratense	Meadow cranesbill
Hieracium maculatum	Spotted hawkweed
Holcus lanatus	Yorkshire fog
Hordeum secalinum	Meadow barley

Botanical name	Common name
Hypericum pulchrum	Slender St John's wort
H. tetrapterum	Square stemmed St John's wort
Hypochoeris radicata	Cat's ear
Jasione montana	Sheepsbit scabious
Knautia arvensis	Field scabious
Leontodon hispidus	Rough hawkbit
Leucanthemum vulgare	Oxeye daisy
Linaria vulgaris	Common toadflax
Lotus corniculatus	Birdsfoot trefoil
Malva moschata	Musk mallow
Medicago lupulina	Black medick
Myosotis arvensis	Field forget-me-not
Papaver rhoeas	Common poppy
Phleum pratense	Timothy
Plantago lanceolata	Ribwort plantain
Poa pratensis	Smooth meadow grass
Primula veris	Cowslip
Prunella vulgaris	Selfheal
Pulicaria dysenterica	Common fleabane
Ranunculus acris	Meadow buttercup
Rhinanthus minor	Yellow rattle
Rumex acetosa	Sorrel
Saxifraga granulata	Meadow saxifrage
Silene alba	White campion
S. conica	Sand catchfly
Trifolium arvense	Haresfoot clover
T. dubium	Suckling clover
T. repens	White clover
Trisetum flavescens	Golden oatgrass
Verbascum thapsus	Great mullein
Verbena officinalis	Vervain
Veronica chamaedrys	Common speedwell
Vicia cracca	Tufted vetch

2. Woodlands

Acer campestre	Field maple
Alnus glutinosa	Alder
Anemone nemorosa	Wood anemone

(continued over)

Botanical name	Common name
Arum maculatum	Lords-and-ladies
Betula pendula	Silver birch
B. pubescens	Downy birch
Carpinus betulus	Hornbeam
Chelidonium majus	Greater celandine
Clematis vitalba	Old man's beard
Cornus sanguinea	Dogwood
Corylus avellana	Hazel
Crataegus monogyna	Hawthorn
C. oxycanthoides	Midland hawthorn
Cytisus scoparius	Broom
Digitalis purpurea	Foxglove
Endymion non-scriptus	Bluebell
Fagus sylvatica	Beech
Fraxinus excelsior	Ash
Galanthus nivalis	Snowdrop
Geranium robertianum	Herb Robert
Ilex aquifolium	Holly
Lamium album	White deadnettle
L. galeobdolon	Yellow archangel
L. purpureum	Red deadnettle
Ligustrum vulgare	Wild privet
Lonicera periclymenum	Honeysuckle
Mercurialis perennis	Dog's mercury
Narcissus pseudonarcissus	Wild daffodil
Primula vulgaris	Primrose
Prunus avium	Gean or wild cherry
P. padus	Bird cherry
P. spinosa	Blackthorn
Quercus petraea	Sessile oak
Q. robur	Common oak
Ranunculus ficaria	Lesser celandine
Rosa canina	Dog rose
Rubus fruticosus	Bramble
Sambucus nigra	Elder
Silene dioica	Red campion
Ulex europaeus	Gorse
Viburnum opulus	Guelder rose
Viola riviniana	Common violet

3. Wetlands

Botanical name	Common name
Alisma plantago-aquatica	Water plantain
Apium nodiflorum	Fool's watercress
Butomus umbellatus	Flowering rush
Callitriche stagnalis	Water starwort
Caltha palustris	Marsh marigold
Carex spp.	Sedges
Ceratophyllum spp.	Hornworts
Epilobium hirsutum	Great hairy willow-herb
Equisetum fluviatile	Water horsetail
Eriophorum spp.	Cotton grasses
Glyceria fluitans	Flote grass
G. maxima	Reed sweet grass
Hippuris vulgaris	Marestail
Hottonia palustris	Water violet
Hydrocharis morsus-ranae	Frog-bit
Iris pseudacorus	Yellow or flag iris
Lemna spp.	Duckweeds
Lychnis flos-cuculi	Ragged robin
Lysimachia vulgaris	Yellow loosestrife
Lythrum salicaria	Purple loosestrife
Mentha aquatica	Water mint
Menyanthes trifoliata	Bog bean
Myosotis scorpioides	Water forget-me-not
Myriophyllum spicatum	Water milfoil
Nuphar lutea	Yellow water-lily
Nymphaea alba	White water-lily
Phalaris arundinacea	Reed canary-grass
Phragmites australis	Common reed
Polygonum amphibium	Amphibious bistort
Potamogeton crispus	Curled pondweed
P. natans	Broad leaved pondweed
P. perfoliatus	Perfoliate pondweed
Potentilla palustris	Marsh cinquefoil
Ranunculus aquatilis	Water crowfoot
R. flammula	Lesser spearwort
R. lingua	Greater spearwort
Rorippa islandica	Marsh yellow-cress

Botanical name	Common name
Rumex hydrolapathum	Great water dock
Sagittaria sagittifolia	Arrowhead
Schoenoplectus lacustris	Bulrush or clubrush
Scirpus martimus	Sea club-rush
Sparganium emersum	Unbranched bur-reed
S. erectum	Branched bur-reed
Stachys palustris	Marsh woundwort
Typha angustifolia	Lesser reedmace
T. latifolia	Reedmace
Veronica beccabunga	Brooklime

4. Wastelands

Botanical name	Common name
Agrostemma githago	Corncockle
Agrostis stolonifera	Creeping bent
Anagallis arvensis	Scarlet pimpernel
Artemisia vulgaris	Mugwort
Buddleja davidii	Buddleja
Capsella bursa-pastoris	Shepherd's purse
Cerastium holosteoides	Common mouse-ear
Chamerion angustifolium	Rosebay willowherb
Chenopodium album	Fat-hen
Chrysanthemum segetum	Corn marigold
Cichorium intybus	Chicory
Cirsium arvense	Creeping thistle
Dactylis glomerata	Cocksfoot
Epilobium adenocaulon	American willow herb
Euphorbia peplus	Petty spurge
Lamium purpureum	Red deadnettle
Matricaria matricarioides	Pineapple mayweed
Papaver rhoeas	Common poppy
Poa annua	Annual meadow grass
Polygonum aviculare	Knotgrass
P. persicaria	Redshanks
Potentilla anserina	Silverweed
Ranunculus repens	Creeping buttercup
Rumex crispus	Curled dock
Senecio squalidus	Oxford ragwort
S. vulgaris	Groundsel
Sisymbrium officinale	Hedge mustard
Sonchus oleraceus	Smooth sowthistle

Botanical name	Common name
Spergula arvensis	Corn spurrey
Stellaria media	Common chickweed
Thlaspi arvense	Field penny-cress
Tussilago farfara	Coltsfoot
Urtica dioica	Common nettle
Veronica persica	Field speedwell

Chris Baines B.Sc. Hort. (Wye), Dip L.A. (Birm), A.L.I. (Management), M.I. Biol.

Chris Baines is a horticulturist and landscape architect who has worked in the landscape contracting industry, municipal parks and international landscape consultancy. He has advised both government departments and local authorities. He taught landscape design and management at the City of Birmingham Polytechnic for 15 years and, in 1988, was awarded a personal professorship.
Now he is best known as an environmental writer and broadcaster. *The Wild Side of Town* (book and TV programme) and *Bluetits and Bumblebees – the Making of a Wildlife Garden* (TV) have been particularly influential.
Chris was a founder, and first elected Chairman, of the Urban Wildlife Group, is Vice-Chair of the British Wildlife Appeal, and is a Member of Council of the Royal Society for Nature Conservation and the World Wide Fund for Nature (UK).

Jane Smart Ph.D. (Sheffield)

Jane Smart is a plant ecologist who has carried out research into the rehabilitation of wetlands for nature conservation, in association with the Nature Conservancy Council. As part of the Greater London Council's Ecology Section, and later the London Ecology Unit, she was responsible for the provision of technical advice on the creation and management of habitats. She then worked for the London Wildlife Trust as its Conservation Director. Jane is now Director of the new charity, Plantlife, of which she was a founder member.